COMING HOME

A MANUAL FOR SPIRITUAL DIRECTION

by
Betsy Caprio
and
Thomas M. Hedberg, S.D.B.

PAULIST PRESS
New York/Mahwah

Library of Congress
Catalog Card Number: 85-61739

ISBN: 0-8091-2787-3

Published by Paulist Press
997 Macarthur Boulevard
Mahwah, N.J. 07430

Printed and bound in the United States of America

Contents

Introduction

This book is a manual to accompany COMING HOME—a handbook for those who want to explore their inner worlds along religious and psychological lines, particularly in the vein of the psychology of C.G. Jung. In this companion volume are thoughts and aids for those *who travel with* inner explorers as spiritual companions or spiritual directors; the material also will be useful to those in many of the other "walking with others" ministries: prayer partner; retreat director; formation director; pastoral counselor; religious psychologist; spiritually-oriented therapist; sponsor; religious educator; and, most important, parent.

The spiritual guide's goal is to help those who come to him or to her to deepen their relationship to God, for the very core of the western religions is the vision of a life of intimate union with one's creator. It is this sacred relationship that the spiritual companion is privileged to facilitate, knowing all the while that the spirit of God is the real director or guide. Another way to say this is to use the language of prayer: as each of us draws nearer and nearer to our God, our prayer becomes more and more the prayer of union. The companion on the spiritual journey supports and encourages this deepening in the pilgrim's prayer life.

It is suggested that the basic book, COMING HOME, be given to those who come for spiritual guidance, with the suggestion that they dip into it at random, pausing to read and do the journal exercises wherever they like. The journal pages can be brought to the direction session, and shared as fully as the person who has done them cares to. After the relationship between inner journeyer and companion has been established, a next step might be the check-list included in the journal pages for Chapter Five of COMING HOME. Together, the two can go over this assessment list and focus on a couple of areas which seem to be most important at this time in the pilgrim's life. (Prayer is always the core of the direction material, no matter how many

other interesting and valuable spiritual practices are grouped around it.)

The spiritual director will already have his or her own style of working with others, which may be supplemented by the initial thoughts in this manual, focusing on how Jung's psychology can inform our efforts in this ministry. Here, too, the basic theories underpinning COMING HOME are amplified so that the guide has a conceptual frame of reference for the chapters of the book. We have repeated the chart that shows, in simple form, the correspondence between the conversion process we speak of in religious language and Jung's individuation process. Also included is a broad listing of symbols that express the theory, for these come up over and over when one is "going fishing" in the waters of the unconscious.

The user of this manual will also find some sample handouts which can be copied and given to those coming for guidance as needed. It's important not to overload someone who may spend only one hour a month with a spiritual guide; there is material here for many months of shared exploration.

Some pitfalls for both directors and "directees" are noted, and the manual closes with a description of a specific spiritual direction and growth center. This illustrates the way in which the authors and others have attempted to put all these theoretical ideas into practice, and may help the reader further concretize the contents of COMING HOME and this manual.

It is our hope that those who are privileged to share the spiritual odysseys of others will find the pages that follow useful aids for themselves and the others who are coming home—to the kingdom of heaven within each of us.

Thomas M. Hedberg, S.D.B.
Betsy Caprio

Los Angeles

The Changing Ministry of Spiritual Direction

There was a time when the name "spiritual director" had a very specific picture attached to it: the phrase called up the guider of souls for a religious community of men or women, almost always a priest. A beard, preferably grey, was usually included in the image of spiritual director within us— a somewhat modified version of a bearded and sage God the Father. Direction usually took place as part of the sacrament of reconciliation, and was largely devoted to:

- a scrutiny of one's prayer life

- an examen of the faults which plagued one and which were (one hoped) in the process of being rooted out.

Yes, there were a few other pictures which could come up when one heard "spiritual director": one of these was the desert father or mother in a cave or the occasional Catherine or Teresa to whom people made pilgrimages for sage advice. Another was that of the court confessor or holy bishop of a European city, sought out by the well-to-do who wanted a deeper life in Christ.

While each of these modes of spiritual direction was, indeed, focused on Jesus, their Christocentricity did not save many of them from going far afield from the simplicity and loving acceptance of Jesus himself. There are exceptions, to be sure, but for the most part the tone of the writing about and practicing spiritual direction over the last four hundred years in the church of the west has overtones of hard work and watchfulness for sin; this is

our Puritan, Jansenist, Counter Reformation heritage.[1]

The second half of the twentieth century has seen a renewal occur in the ministry of spiritual direction. The Roman Catholic Second Vatican Council, seed-bed of hope for a return to the truest nature of Jesus, has been one of the largest factors behind this change. Underlying this shape-shifting are key names, like Merton and Lewis, Teilhard and Thérèse of France, whose head ached when she had to say long prayers. We have rediscovered their spiritual ancestors: hesychasts of the eastern church, medieval mystics along the Rhine and across the sea in Britain, earlier Celtic Christians as much connected with the flow of the Tao as any ancient of China—and sharing that in intricately woven illuminated manuscripts.[2]

True, traditional spiritual direction as we have described it above is still alive and healthy—but side by side with it lives a renewal of this more personal, mystical tradition with its unifying thread of hunger for the immanence of God. For the mystic and the prophet as for Jesus, God lives in one's heart, in one's daily surroundings, in one's intimate connections to others. This second great strand of Christian asceticism has been affecting the ministry of spiritual direction in our time, and, in all likelihood, will continue to influence its style even more as we move toward the two thousandth year of our Lord.

Paralleling this renewed interest in our personal-relationship-with-God ancestors is the century's very own science, psychology. Increased psychological sophistication, on the part of both director and directee, is perhaps the second most important factor in the sea-change in spiritual direction. And it is depth psychology which has had the most to say about the soul, most strikingly the depth psychology or analytical psychology of C.G. Jung. From the earliest days of Jung's writings, in the 1920's, his work was taken up, argued, built on or rejected by the religious community. The great names of each decade had their say, most notably, Victor White and Martin Buber in the 1950's. In the 1980's, Roman Catholic priest and Jungian analyst John P. Dourley has given us penetrating insight into the congruency of Jung's thought with that of Paul Tillich's, most notably in a paper titled "Jung, Tillich, and the Quest for Home and Self."[3]

It is largely in the practical climate of the American culture that the people have sprung up who bridge religion and psychology: Powell, Kunkel, Kennedy, Nouwen, van Kaam, Muto, Fox, Edwards, May,[4] and the specifically Jung-oriented religious teachers and writers: Kelsey, Sanford, Johnson, Ulanov, Progoff, Welch, Howes and Moon and the others who for many years have furthered this marriage at San Francisco's Guild for Psychological Studies, Clift,and Abbot David Geraets and the Pecos, New Mexico Community.[5]

Still another change upon the spiritual direction scene is the increased calling-out of believers for the person who can be spiritual companion or guide. As lay people's spiritual awareness has heightened, this sort of helper has been more and more in demand. Not finding trained guides in the institutional religions, many turn to spiritually oriented therapists or analysts, to spiritual astrologers, to whomever they can find. (Abraham Maslow called such people from the secular helping professions "metacounselors," counselors about that which is *meta*—changed or beyond.)

The charismatic renewal, particularly, has created a hunger for the one-to-one guidance which comparatively few lay people sought some twenty years ago. Leaders of prayer groups have found themselves in this role with little or no training, scrambling to get a handle on yet another ministry. The diminishing numbers of clergy in the Roman Catholic Church (which, as Tilden Edwards points out, has been the traditional home of spiritual direction as a ministry)[6] has created even more of a gap in the ranks, for it was to the clergy that most people used to turn for guidance . . . in the old days.

But these are the new days . . . and we live in a time when the challenging and humbling ministry of spiritual direction—and all the other "walking with others" ministries—are in a flux. For those who find themselves called to this art form, a knowledge of their predecessors is indispensable, as is reflection upon the widely varying styles of direction so that one may find one's own unique way. This way will be influenced, of course, by our own training, but also by things like our ethnic roots and our typology and the breadth of our general education, even the sort of art we find most nourishing to the soul.[7] (One of the authors recalls going to three training programs in one year on spiritual guiding; in each, the assumption was made and never stated that spiritual direction equated with the Ignatian method of direction . . . yet this is only one way of several.) Let's take a look now, specifically, at...

Spiritual Direction From a Jungian Approach[8]

C.G. Jung was very clear about the absolute importance of soul-exploring being done with the help of the well-trained guide. He transformed Freud's model of the analyst-patient (on couch) relationship to one of face-to-face dialogue, in which the guide enters the soul-life of the one being guided, and goes along with him or her as they meet the contents of the unconscious. It is no secret to Jung and his followers that whoever comes to their offices to do the inner work is sent for *their* own growing and development as well. Jungian analysis is a two-way street; both parties are affected, just as two chemical substances brought together either remain as they are or *both* change.

The same is true in spiritual direction; the analytical model can be translated. However, we are not practicing Jungian analysis; we are talking about Christian spiritual direction from a Jung-influenced point of view . . . and there are differences between these two ways of sharing another's journey. The biggest difference (and the most comforting for the helper) is that in spiritual direction we know it is God doing the directing, not ourselves. This is certainly implied in Jung's thought; the good analyst follows the clues sent by the other's inner image of God, the Self, as it strives to become realized in that person's life. Yet the spiritual director will have a freedom to talk about how God is leading the person that the analyst may not have; the spiritual director can and must pray with and for the persons who come, and has their lifetime or years of religious practice in a collective way on which to build the individual work. All of these specifically religious assets give the spiritual director a framework of support that goes beyond "just" the meeting of two psyches or souls.

Let's list some of the qualities of spiritual direction when it is practiced from a Jungian point of view; most of these have been alluded to throughout the text of COMING HOME, but it may help to synthesize them here. By no means are these qualities exclusive to this style of guiding; they have deep roots in our past asceticism as well. We will see that they place us firmly in the more personal tradition of Christian spirituality which we spoke of earlier as enjoying a renaissance. Then we will need to be specific about the gaps in Jung's thought of which the Jung-oriented spiritual director needs to be aware.

Spiritual Direction from a Jungian Viewpoint Tends To Be:	The Implications of This Tendency for the Director's Style:
1. *Very Inner-Directed:* God is seen as living within us: "the Kingdom of Heaven is within." God doesn't lead us all by the same plan, but uniquely and individually.	1. Helps one discern what God is calling one to at this time, as though holding up a mirror to reflect back what is there—rather than suggesting many exercises or procedures (although there may be "assignments").
2. *The Inner World/Spiritual World* is a reality, just as much as the outer world. Spiritual growth is seen as a dialogue between the part of the spiritual world which is already conscious, and that which is unconscious.	2. Asks one what the unconscious is saying, what clues about growth are being sent.
3. *Little or No Distinction Between "Religious" and "Secular,"* because all of life is seen as sacred. "Religious" doesn't mean only churchy things; it means all of one's life that has connection to the God within.	3. Encourages one to bring one's entire life to direction: prayer, yes, and also relationships, hopes and dreams, fears and foibles, little things. Importance is measured by the amount of affect the matter generates, not by how "holy" it is.
4. *Failings/Sin/Examining One's Conscience* do not play a *large* part (this is not to say they are done away with completely). Requesting spiritual direction indicates a fundamental choice for life with God; the source of unwholeness or brokenness therefore is most often viewed as unconsciousness or as what one needs to draw to him/herself, rather than deliberate sinfulness.	4. Very *unlikely* to exhort one to "work on correcting your predominant fault," because aware that as consciousness increases, "faults" (unconscious contents) come into daylight and fade in the sun (only for new ones to be revealed!).
5. *Very Visual (Right Brain, Kataphatic).* Language of the soul is visual, rather than verbal. This is the language of the child within, the primitive within. It is the language which all peoples speak and understand; it unites us to others.	5. Encourages one to discover personal symbols, draw, sculpt, collect pictures, use colors, etc. Tells stories to directees, likely to suggest movies and t.v. programs as part of one's *sadhana* (spiritual practices).
6. *The Inner Work Takes Time, Requires a Commitment*—which may mean reprioritizing one's whole life. Interior life is not just one of many good things, but THE most important thing: "Seek ye first the kingdom of God."	6. Will probably be very selective in whom he or she spends guiding-time with. Expects dream logging and, probably, journal-keeping and active imagination efforts on one's own. Also, fidelity to regularity in meetings. Person being guided supplies the material for the sessions (rather, God within the person does this).
7. *Material for Spiritual Growth Will Come From a Wide-Ranging Variety of Sources*—not only the religious tradition of the person but all religions, and cultures old and new, east and west (folklore, art forms, etc.).	7. All kinds of material are brought in to amplify one's experiences, since people of other times and places have had the same inner and outer experiences. Will be encouraging both of ecumenism and transcultural dialogue.

8. *Optimism!* No matter how bad things get, no matter how many abysses and dark nights one goes through, the presumption is that the psyche tends toward healing and wholeness, that God desires the harmonizing of the disparate parts of ourselves.

9. *The Collective* (in this case, the religious institution to which one may belong) is seen as a valuable container, but not as a substitute for one's conscious, individual encounter with God. (This is a great advantage for those caught in the storms of institutional debate; if one identifies totally with the institution, there is great temptation to walk away from it when its leaders become too conservative/liberal for one's taste.)

10. *A Lack of Pie-in-the-Sky-Ness:* The approach described herein will not be particularly attractive to those who like their religion all light and beautiful. The shadow—and the dark side of all the archetypes—is as real as the light (though, more often than not, equally as rich a source of strength).

11. *A Delight* . . . yes, yes, there are the hard times and dark corners, but there is also the joy of seeing someone's truest nature be born. The inner child is allowed to surface, often after a lifetime of neglect—and especially if the director uses aids like a sandtray or drawing materials it is a moment of wonder to see pictures of another's inner world emerge.

8. A hopeful attitude. Through experience, the Jung-oriented guide has learned that when one listens to the unconscious and enters into dialogue with it, rich fruits are harvested. (Some may be bitter fruits, but even they are nourishing.)

9. Will probably challenge one to distinguish between:

   • being *contained by* the church, and expecting it to live out the mysteries for one, and

   • being *related to* the church, with deep appreciation for the way in which her celebration of the sacred mysteries helps one do the same . . . interiorly. (See the comments on Edward Edinger's work later in this manual.)

   Helps the one being guided experience adult conversion, if he or she has not already done so.

10. Knows that when one attitude appears consciously, its opposite is almost surely constellated in the unconscious. Will challenge the person to look at *both* sides; a very inclusive approach.

11. The spiritual director is not only guide and companion, but co-celebrant of one's life, witness to transformation. This is a tremendous privilege, a holy gift *to the guide*. Together, rites of passage can be celebrated.

As mentioned above, none of the points is exclusively true of this style of spiritual direction; most of them have been experienced down through the ages in many formats of this art. The combination of them is, perhaps, what makes spiritual direction from a Jungian-Christian standpoint unique. It is not everyone's way, but for those called to it, there is no other! One of the greatest blessings of both authors' lives has been to see rich fruits of peace, happiness, consciousness—and service—grow abundantly in the lives of those willing to explore their religion inwardly, in the manner we've been describing. It works.

And what are the omissions in analytical psychology from the Christian viewpoint? There are some, and it is important not to fudge over them. Six stand out:

1. The unclear view of Jung himself on the nature of evil, and the question of whether or not God must contain an evil side—since we, made in God's likeness, have such an aspect to our nature. Related to this is the matter of the egocentricity of the ego, and the resulting seemingly "evil" reactions of the Self to that egocentricity, matters tackled in John A. Sanford's work.[9]

2. The gap (for those who belong to a faith community) created by lack of emphasis on the need for others, the concept of the mystical body which is so much a part of Christian thought, especially. There is, underlying Jung's psychology, the substratum of the collective unconscious; in this way, all people of all times and places share in like imagery, feelings, needs, instincts and are thus bound . . . but one misses in the psychology the sense of mutual service and fellowship one is used to in religious settings. As a psychology, it does not concern itself with needs of social justice in the way a religion must

. . . however, this concern is not absent from Jung's thought (see "Sharing Our Home" in Chapter Nine).

3. Another lacuna or empty space is found when we look through the Jungian literature for models, heroes. There is almost the implication that to need such persons in our lives is to want to give away part of ourselves through projecting it onto the hero. In Jungian thought the hero is within; the saint lives in us, waiting to be uncovered; the outer model can be a distraction from the task of finding the higher octave of ourself. True enough . . . yet, again, those used to the tradition of heroes and saints which is common to the world's religions, may miss them when exploring analytical psychology.

Akin to this gap is the possible diminution of Jesus into "just one more hero," one of the thousand faces of the hero—and the story of the incarnation as just one more hero myth. For Christians, of course, this is unacceptable; it ignores the divinity of Jesus and his uniqueness.

4. Also common to the world's religions, for the most part, is some sort of outward revelation; for Jews and Christians that is, primarily, the Bible. With the immense focus on inward revelation in Jung's psychology, we might overlook other, more external and handed-down forms of God's voice, even though Jung himself was a scholar of several aspects of scripture, most notably the Book of Job.

5. For Christians, the fact that God became human is central. The incarnation makes matter holy. In the psychology of C.G. Jung, we miss the attention to the body with which we have become familiar through the more recent psychologies (humanistic and transpersonal). Jung was himself a medical doctor, and this gap in his writing is not a deliberate, Manichaean slight of the flesh but, rather, an oversight. He was caught up in the psyche . . . but we know today how inseparable *psyche* and *soma* are. We need to remember the time and place in which Jung and his immediate followers grew up and worked, a time and place quite different from late twentieth century America or western Europe. Also, Jung's own high degree of intuition indicates a lesser connectedness to sensation, the function which enables us to hear the body's wisdom.

6. Finally, when approaching the life of the soul strictly via the avenue of analytical psychology, we could miss one of the key undercurrents of most of the world's great faiths—and that is the loving nature of God. A God who loves us is much more than a symbolic image of God in the soul; this sort of God implies relationship, joyous and even ecstatic relationship. In the Jungian literature we have hints of it, though: the Self yearns for reconciliation with us, we read. This is the language of religion.[10]

None of the above is in any way meant to detract from the genius of analytical psychology's founder; to take the scientist to task for not being a theologian, as Jung repeatedly complained people were prone to do—and which is something like faulting Babe Ruth for not scoring touchdowns—is to miss the whole point of COMING HOME. What we are about is allowing our ancient faith to be informed by this psychology, which—as Jung with his wealth of religious scholarship amply illustrated—has equally ancient roots. The great contribution of C.G. Jung to our knowledge of the soul is unquestioned, and he himself summed it up best in his autobiography, saying, "The decisive question . . . is, (is one) related to something infinite or not?" Psychologist and theologian can both agree on that.

One Way of Looking at Spiritual Growth

As the summary in the handbook states, COMING HOME has presented an approach to spiritual growth that is most easily pictured by the spiral "maps" of Chapter Four. In simplest form we could describe the process as

1. being at home, but not being aware of that

2. leaving home . . . then, turning around

and

3. returning home, knowingly.

The developmental chart that follows shows the correspondence between the Christian language for this process and the Jungian language. It also gives us some of the scriptural images that tell about each stage of this growth process.

Although drawn in linear form, we should not imagine that everyone proceeds along a smooth growth path!— wouldn't that be nice! There are, so often, roadblocks and regressions all along the way. One may cease development at any point. Nothing about the soul can be described as neatly as a chart would have it . . . but it does give us an overview of the growth process.

It might be helpful to imagine the chart in the form of a tube, with the final right-hand column doubling back to the beginning; this developmental map—as the spiral pictures show us—isn't a one-way road or ladder, as it looks on paper, but a return to what has always been there. This chart is just the spiral map stretched out to fit the pages of a book.

The Life of the Soul	Beginnings ⟶	Normal Life ⟶
The Conversion Process: "I" and "Thou"	Little children are naturally in a state of union with God . . . although they may not know it. We celebrate this with **baptism.**	Mainstreamed into life of institution/group; celebrated in sacramental churches by **first penance and eucharist.** Part of church because of parents, then out of habit . . . or fear, or need for security. Unconscious identification with the collective group.
The Individuation Process: "I" and "Not-I" (Or Self)	We are born with the "map" of totality already complete . . . in a pre-conscious unitive state. No sense of "I" or "me" (pre-ego). all is one ◯ (*participation mystique*) —no consciousness— Erich Neumann's UROBORIC STAGE,[11] after Uroborus, the ancient circular image of the serpent biting its own tail	*Individuation: Part 1* Sense of "I" (ego) begins to emerge from womb-like state, though still contained by it. (Neumann's MATRIARCHAL STAGE) 3 stages postulated by Kalff: • animal-vegetative (still very instinctual) • fighting to break out • adaptation to the collective (Neumann's PATRIARCHAL STAGE) *May* make it = healthy ego ("the hero") OR *May not* make it = ego remains weak, and compensates by defenses (Kunkel)[12] and/or seeking new substitute "womb"
The Story of Salvation (Salvation History)★	Creation of the World Paradise Prodigal son at home	Kingdom of Israel——— Promised Land——— Jerusalem, the holy city——— Goes away——— Grain of wheat——— "I live . . ."——— "The people who—

★The reader will find many more scriptural (and other) examples of this process under "The Journey or Transformation Image" on page 18.

Note that throughout this book and the chart there are two circular diagrams, not to be confused:
• the spiral pictures, which are the map of the growth process itself;
• the mandalic pictures, which show the soul as it *goes through* the growth process (above), and in their simplest form show the beginning and end of the growth process.

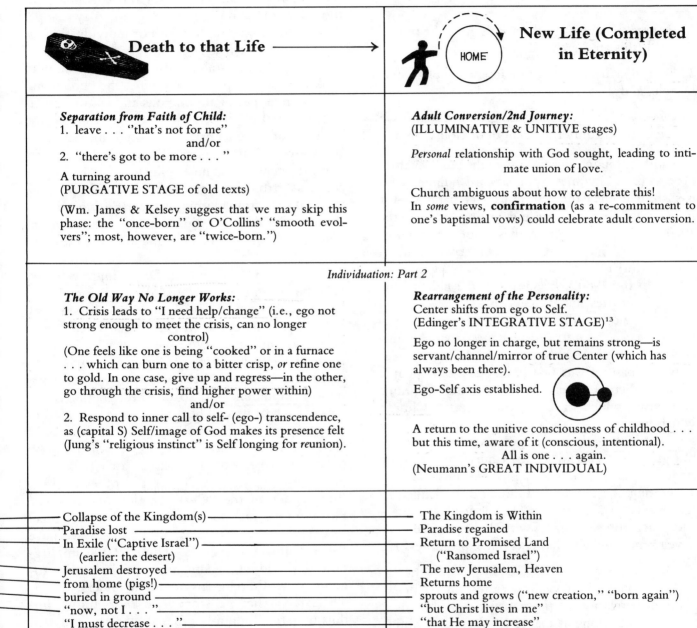

Death to that Life ——————→

New Life (Completed in Eternity)

HOME

Separation from Faith of Child:
1. leave . . . "that's not for me"
                                    and/or
2. "there's got to be more . . . "

A turning around
(PURGATIVE STAGE of old texts)

(Wm. James & Kelsey suggest that we may skip this phase: the "once-born" or O'Collins' "smooth evolvers"; most, however, are "twice-born.")

Adult Conversion/2nd Journey:
(ILLUMINATIVE & UNITIVE stages)

Personal relationship with God sought, leading to intimate union of love.

Church ambiguous about how to celebrate this!
In *some* views, **confirmation** (as a re-commitment to one's baptismal vows) could celebrate adult conversion.

Individuation: Part 2

The Old Way No Longer Works:
1. Crisis leads to "I need help/change" (i.e., ego not strong enough to meet the crisis, can no longer control)
(One feels like one is being "cooked" or in a furnace . . . which can burn one to a bitter crisp, *or* refine one to gold. In one case, give up and regress—in the other, go through the crisis, find higher power within)
                                    and/or
2. Respond to inner call to self- (ego-) transcendence, as (capital S) Self/image of God makes its presence felt (Jung's "religious instinct" is Self longing for *reunion*).

Rearrangement of the Personality:
Center shifts from ego to Self.
(Edinger's INTEGRATIVE STAGE)[13]

Ego no longer in charge, but remains strong—is servant/channel/mirror of true Center (which has always been there).

Ego-Self axis established.

A return to the unitive consciousness of childhood . . . but this time, aware of it (conscious, intentional).
                    All is one . . . again.
(Neumann's GREAT INDIVIDUAL)

— Collapse of the Kingdom(s) ———————— The Kingdom is Within
— Paradise lost ———————— Paradise regained
— In Exile ("Captive Israel") ———————— Return to Promised Land
        (earlier: the desert)   ("Ransomed Israel")
— Jerusalem destroyed ———————— The new Jerusalem, Heaven
— from home (pigs!) ———————— Returns home
— buried in ground ———————— sprouts and grows ("new creation," "born again")
— "now, not I . . ." ———————— "but Christ lives in me"
— "I must decrease . . ." ———————— "that He may increase"
— walk in darkness . . ." ———————— "have seen a great light"
— "Heart of stone," "hardness of ♥ " ———————— "become as little children"

---

n.b. This chart is *not* age-specific; and one can stop at any point

ONE CAN MOVE ALONG:
a. With the group or collective
b. On the solo path
c. Both (b. has priority)

A similar breakdown of stages is postulated by John Sanford, who in work based on that of Professor Alan Jones of General Theological Seminary in New York, and as yet unpublished, suggests three stages of Christian conversion—each preceded by a crisis—that represent an emergence from the "normal life" to a life of wellness and Self-centeredness. He cites the crises of

1. *the need for meaning* (our "there's got to be more" or "is this all there is?"),

2. *betrayal,* when we have to accept the unacceptable, and

3. *absence,* when there is no thing/one on which we can lean . . . only the strength of God within.

Another, longer, description of the individuation process (part 2) comes from Edward Edinger who has studied the story of Jesus—its parallel—for many years, first speaking and writing on this in the 1960's and then collecting these thoughts for *Ego and Archetype,* published in 1972, in the well-known essay "Christ as Paradigm of the Individuating Ego." In the 1980's, he speaks in the light of the span of centuries and even epochs.

Breaking down the story of Jesus—"the Christian archetype"—into fifteen stages from Annunciation to the Last Judgment, Dr. Edinger traces how this pattern was first lived out by the people of Israel, then, uniquely, by Jesus. In the two thousand years which have elapsed, it is the Church which has lived out the pattern for most of us, he says, celebrating these passages in sacred art and the liturgical year. *And,* when the Church lives out the stages, it can provide a safeguard against our encountering the psychical dying and its dangers—but it may also deprive us of experiencing the archetypal realm personally, with all the possibility of development which that encounter promotes. He says,

> " . . . (one) will have no need to find . . . individual relation to the transpersonal dimension . . . (as long as that task is) done for him by the Church."[14]

In our day, thanks largely to the affirmation of the reality of the unconscious which has become part of our world-view since Freud and Jung, more and more people do set out to encounter the archetypal realm personally. COMING HOME and the many books footnoted therein and herein (as well as the entire body of what we might call "human potential literature" which has inundated us since the 1960's) encourages us to do just that . . . with proper safeguards, the most important of which is the trained and experienced guide, someone who has been there. The inward journey may be taken as a response to a call—or, it may be forced on us by crisis . . . or both of these initiations may happen. Those who belong to a religious group find that it can provide a vessel for this encounter, although our relationship to that group may change. We needn't choose either faith or individuation, as some writers seem to suggest.

There have, of course, always been those who took the "solo trip" to the divine, the known and unknown heroes of all religious and cultural traditions (and also, those who have encountered the contents of the unconscious through mental instability—we call it "madness," but it is not very far from the state of the inner pilgrim. The latter person has a strong enough ego to deal with the surging contents from within; the person who breaks down under their eruption does not. One is an intentional encounter with the unconscious; the other accidental).

The epoch now dawning, Dr. Edinger believes, will be a time of more and more individuals throughout the world living out the Christian story *personally*. This is the way in which C.G. Jung's new myth, of which we have written, will be experienced—the imitation of Christ by many—as individuals go through their own Annunciation, their own Temptation, and so on through the Christ story. Each of us will be invited to the creation of consciousness, the re-collecting of the sparks of God's life loosed among us—and we will do this by taking the journey of the Christian archetypal story ourselves. Truly, we will then be "other Christs" (Jung spoke of the "Christification of many").[15] Furthermore, one does not have to be a Christian to experience this pattern, for it is—as we have seen—a universal pattern. Think of the implications of this idea for ecumenism and the coming together of world religions in mutual understanding. The same archetypal story is to be found in Hinduism, in the Buddhist faith, for Moslems and even for those who still practice the old nature religions of primitive peoples. It is to be found in the lives of those who practice no religion, as well.

Our chart shows the individuation process. It shows us going out of and then coming back to the inner home. We are entering a time, we believe (along with Dr. Edinger and Thomas Merton, and many, many others), when it will be essential for each of us to travel to that eternal home within.

(See also the endnotes for still another parallel developmental map from the Pali Buddhist tradition.)

How does it help the spiritual guide to have an understanding of this process? Well, it's essential that one guiding others have a clear picture of where there is to go—and how one gets there. For all the negativity of the old ascetical theology, the three-step stage-theory of purgation, illumination and union (which dates back to patristic times) was very useful in its envisioning of a goal. Unfortunately, it also implies that the goal is at the end of a ladder or staircase to heaven—the holy *scala* of John Climacus and others—rather than a return to something that has always been. The person who guides others will want to ask himself or herself questions like:

- Do I see spiritual growth as an ascent (of Mt. Carmel, perhaps) or in the spiral way pictured above? What are the implications of my view of spiritual growth in a direction situation?—do I urge persons onward and upward? or do I speak to them of finding something which has always been there, but has gotten covered over? Which image did Jesus use?

- Since both of the above traditions—spiritual growth as a ladder to climb and spiritual growth as a reclaiming of that which is lost—are scripturally rooted, can I share with those who come to me Scripture that reflects my view of spiritual growth?

- Has my view of spiritual growth taken root in my own life? For example, although I may find the spiraling home map appealing and assent to it as my model, I may really live out of a linear mentality that would have one leave earth and matter behind as one ascends to the stars. (This, at its extreme, is a denial of the incarnation; it is a stance that has continually cropped up in the history of the church and been labeled as heretical—yet it lives today.) Not all ladders deny creation; some, like Jacob's, connect heaven and earth, affirming both.

- What image of *myself* have I when engaged in the ministry of spiritual direction? Am I a midwife, perhaps, or someone helping to polish a beautiful creation into its most perfected form? Paul says to the early Corinthians, in effect, "Don't you know who you are?"; he sees their beauty that is hidden even from their own eyes. He also says—to the same Corinthians—"Run the good race, so as to win!", sending them a completely different message that says they have to do something, go

somewhere, rather than just discover what already is. If I connect more with Paul's second quote, above, perhaps my image of myself as director of souls is coach, or guide, or inspirer.

So, the one who would walk with others needs some idea of both the "what" it is he or she is trying to do, and the "how" that happens. Not all see this in the same way; we can summon up worthy witnesses to testify on behalf of more than one approach to spiritual growth. In COMING HOME, we are subscribing to a very centripetal or centroverted map of growth, not saying it is the only way . . . but it is our way.

A second value of our having the spiral map is that it helps us honor a person's growth process which is unfolding at its own pace—at God's pace, really. In the "old days" those coming for spiritual guidance would be apt to hear "do not think of yourself" and/or "you must die that God may live," or words to that effect. We have learned from many of the psychologies how vital it is for a person to have a healthy sense of self (or ego) *before* that can be transcended. An essential stage of individuation is that the locus of both one's *affirmation* and *behavior* move from without to within.

If people come to us who are struggling with self-esteem (and is this not the norm, rather than the exception?), our task as spiritual companions must be to help them treasure their own person and life *before* we talk about giving it away to that which is greater. Faith is developmental, as James Fowler and others have reminded us. We have to take people as we find them—which doesn't mean we can't indicate the goal of spiritual development, just that people start at square one and have to move from there. *Occasionally,* we meet someone who really has been brought along quickly by grace, like Paul being zapped on the road to Damascus; this is as rare, we believe, as oak trees growing overnight from acorns. Spiritual growth, our tradition shows us, takes time; we can move no faster than either grace or nature.

Two Patterns in the Life of the Soul

In Chapter Nine of COMING HOME we discussed two archetypal patterns that appear in the life of the soul as it develops—or, to use the Jungian language, as we become more conscious. Both are present in the spiral map of our own microcosmos, just as they are in the larger macrocosmos, all of creation. Both designs are built into nature and underlie it. Let's look at them again, seeing how they complement each other, and—most important—what the practical implications of this theory are when working with another as spiritual guide.

PATTERN 1	PATTERN 2

THE PATTERN OF WHOLENESS, TOTALITY
or, the Central Archetype

Most often expressed as the *MANDALA*

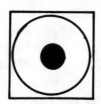

and derivatives of the mandala:

—the set-apart space or container, the *temenos*

—the quaternity or fourfold image

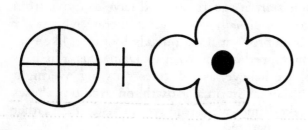

This pattern tells us where we have come from and where we are going. It is a picture of the goal of spiritual growth, God's perfection imprinted in us which strives for realization. It pictures the harmony that comes about when things are in balance.

> " . . . that you may be entire and complete, lacking nothing . . . "
>
> —Jn. 1:4

THE PATTERN OF CHANGE
or the Archetype of Transformation

Most often expressed as the *JOURNEY*, which can be seen as:

—going out:

—going up:

—going in:

—going down:

and can be divided into stages, such as Birth, Life, Death to that Life, Rebirth to a New Life.

This pattern is about how we reach the goal. It answers the question "what am I doing here?" I am a pilgrim, a traveler.

> " . . . if you would be perfect(ed) . . . come, follow me . . . "
>
> —Matt. 19:24

As we noted in Chapter Nine of COMING HOME, the mandalic pattern is representative of the feminine energy in the soul: that energy which holds and waits; the journeying pattern is representative of the masculine energy in the soul: that energy which reaches out and goes somewhere and does something. When they come together in a balanced way in us—that is, when we have both somewhat realized and flowing—there can be the inner marriage, the union of opposites, the *conjunctio*.

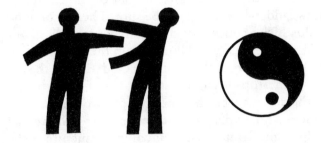

This is an ever-deepening relationship, the process repeats and repeats just as in a successful outer marriage of man and woman . . . and from it (just as in outward life) comes new life, the new creation. In human terms, a new way of being John or Jane or whoever we are comes about when the masculine and feminine energies in ourselves join in happy union; this new creation is the shiny person of Chapter Eight of COMING HOME, made little less than the angels.

The ancient myth of Psyche and Eros illustrates the images above. The male and female protagonists each had to mature (although, since the story is more Psyche's than Eros' or Amor, as he is also known, we hear more about her development than his). Only when they each had developed could they come together to celebrate their nuptial banquet and "live happily every after," and produce their child . . . which is given the name Pleasure.[16]

Very interesting theory, you say! But what does it all mean in terms of spiritual direction? Good question! Let's recap: we are postulating a theory of spiritual growth that is about a home base from which we start, which we leave, and which we then turn toward from a distance and return to. Under-

lying the spiral map of spiritual growth we are using are the two basic patterns: the static one, the moving one. Both are present within our souls. That means they are going to continue to manifest themselves in our lives . . . and if we pay attention to these manifestations, we will know what our next task and then our next focus and the next is in our spiritual unfolding.

To give an example (a very common one): Arthur dreams of himself quite frequently as a marathon runner. When he first began having such dreams, the running seemed to be satisfying. Sometimes he would win the race, or at least place. For the past year, however, he usually dreams of himself beginning the race, then running out of gas, dropping farther and farther behind in the pack of runners, usually waking before he crosses the finish line.

The early dreams would indicate that the moving on, journeying energy in Arthur was well-constellated and serving him; if it enables him to finish the race, even to win the race, it is working for him (the dream language would seem to say). The spiritual guide who worked with Arthur and his dreams would help him note the change in them; now the journeying energy isn't enough, it doesn't satisfy—in fact, it exhausts. Perhaps the dreams are a manifestation of Arthur's outer life as well as the state of his soul. Like so many of us, he may be always on the move, with increasingly long lists of projects through which to race. The series of dreams would indicate to the careful observer that there was a lopsidedness in Arthur's life, a one-sided adaptation with an overabundance of masculine energy driving the psyche.

What might the guide suggest? Going back to our theory—which, of course, is not ours but can be found both in C.G. Jung's work and in the thought of more than one ancient civilization—it would seem that Arthur's life cries out for some of the opposite energy, the quieter, more still, "feminine" energy. One might suggest to him that he increase his time alone each day; if he has no unscheduled time in his calendar, that might be added; if his style of prayer reads like something out of an army boot camp manual, he might be encouraged to try centering prayer. This latter is often enhanced by focusing on some mandalic pattern—there are many Christian mandalas as well as ones from nature, and also abstract patterns that are centering devices.

Of course, the intuitive spiritual guide might come up with suggestions like this *without* a comprehension of spiral maps and underlying patterns in the psyche (in fact, there's probably no one who comes for spiritual direction for whom the above suggestions to slow down wouldn't bear fruit). Spiritual direction, again, is an art far more than a science. We're suggesting that awareness of the theory of the basic movements in the psyche *helps us to be more conscious* in our ministry to others, and certainly in our own inner exploring. One of the basic guidelines of *all* approaches to spiritual direction is that we can take no one farther than we have been ourselves.

The balancing out of energies in the inner life has the fancy name of *enantiodromia,* from the Greek words for opposite and for running; the energy of the soul tends to "run toward the opposite" or "sets the opposite in motion," just as the swing of a clock pendulum to one side propels it to its other extreme.[17] The theory is very old; its application is new each time we encourage inclusiveness rather than one-sidedness in someone we are accompanying spiritually. Throughout COMING HOME the reader is encouraged to develop a "both-and" mentality rather than an "either-or" approach to many facets of inner and outer life.

So, when journeying has been done a great deal, stability and repose cannot be far behind; and the same is true of other pairs of opposites:

- Separating and breaking apart, or dismemberment, needs to be balanced with gathering in, pulling together, and re-membering

- Searching for, and appreciating what already is—both are needed

- Being in touch with heights cannot last forever—its complement, coming down to earth, is just as important

- Apartness and soloness has its time, as does community and intimacy

- Being in charge is necessary, but no more so than surrender.

The list could go on endlessly; we might do well to make up our own list of how we have seen the need for balance forced upon us in our own inner and outer life. This will help us support that same tendency to homeostasis in those with whom we walk. Perhaps, as we do that, we will hear Qoheleth saying "For everything there is a season," or a voice closer to our own time singing Pete Seeger's

" . . . a time to plant, a time to reap . . . "

Our awareness of the soul's need for balance will also help us provide that when those with whom we work bring lop-sided images of God or incomplete models of church to their sessions. God is, indeed, the God of the pilgrimage, but is also the God of the still, small voice within. And, sophisticated as we may be about models of the church, not a week will go by in the average spiritual guide's sitting room which doesn't contain testimony to the power of the institutional model of the church, a very ladder-like image, to be sure. The person who holds such a concept of church may even talk all our collegial language and know from the collar up that church is, indeed, the people of God . . . but the old from-the-top-down mentality about church and authority may be the one living deep inside. The guide who understands the need for balance can help to moderate such an incomplete picture as the two move along together.[18]

There is yet one more value to our having a sense of the two basic patterns of the psyche, and that is we can then better understand the language used by the psyche—the language of symbols. Below are examples of some of the more common ways each of the two basic patterns is expressed symbolically, and also typical symbols of the joining or marriage of the masculine and feminine energies in us, and of the new creation they produce. These images will come up again and again in our life and the lives of others—in sleeping and waking dreams, in projected form. When one of them calls out strongly, it's most helpful to understand to what it might be referring.

Three things to remember about working with the languages of images:

- we can evaluate the importance of a symbol in the psyche by the amount of feeling or affect it generates;

- the appearance of an image does not necessarily mean that what it represents has been made conscious, but only that our *need* for whatever it represents is strong (e.g. a dream that might show us witnessing a wedding of a bride and a groom; this says "this is what you need to attend to" rather than "this is where you are");

- any symbol can have many meanings, depending upon its context, one's associations to it and other factors.

Special Symbols
of the Soul

Here are lists of images of the two great archetypal patterns of the soul, images that call us from without and within. Following these are other symbols that illustrate the fruits of the union of the feminine and the masculine. The journeying pattern is so rich that an additional section on it follows to close this portion of the manual.

Some Symbols of Wholeness and Totality

THE MANDALA: wheel, flying saucer, circle dance, rose window, Uroborous (the serpent biting its own tail), zodiac, solar system, King Arthur's round table, spider in web, kaleidoscope, sand dollar and some other shells, merry-go-round and ferris wheel, Navajo sand painting, compass, chakras (energy centers of body), flowers opening from center, trees viewed from top (especially palm, evergreens), tree cross-section rings, snowflake, eye, ring, crystal cross-section

and Spheres: earth, planets, ball, globe, bubble, marble, sun, round fruit or vegetable, round stone or rock (and especially, precious gems: diamond, pearl, etc.)

and Set-Apart (Temenos) Spaces: tower, lighthouse, church, temple, monastery, cloister, sanctuary, tabernacle, holy of holies, holy ground (as around the burning bush), sacred grove of trees, circle of stones (Stonehenge), womb, island, walled city, enclosed garden, labyrinthe, prayer rug, fountain, animal spaces (beehive, dog house, special corner, shell of crab, turtle, snail, etc.), the body,

Some Symbols of Change and Transformation

THE JOURNEY
Going Out: pilgrim setting off on quest, astronauts going out to explore space, explorers going to uncharted lands (Columbus et al., pioneers in New World), runner of race, leaving home, going off to seek fortune, leaving the world behind

Going Up: climbing stairs, climbing mountain (may be imitation—step up to sanctuary of church; ziggurat or pyramid), climbing tree (cf. Kabbalah) climbing ladder (layers of color in rainbow, working up the body's chakras), flying

Going In: entering a dark place, entering water/swimming, carving wood or stone away from image already there, exploring areas of a dwelling ("in my Father's house are many mansions"), going into hibernation or cocoon, opening treasure chest/Pandora's box/shell with pearl

Going Down: fishing ("let down your nets"), deep-sea diving/excavating, digging for buried treasure/archaeology, sinking into swamp, min-

center of the body (heart-space), chalice, ciborium, pyramid, storage room (with old and new things: Jesus' example), secret hiding place, pages of a book or journal between covers, closed vehicles (train, car, ship, dirigible, spaceship, carriage), home (and center of home: shrine or altar, hearth, furnace), atrium, cell, room of one's own, Walden, Eden, peninsula, ark, houseboat, trailer, consulting room, sandtray, paper or canvas for drawing, treasure chest, tent, egg, cave, coffin, tomb—even a bonded relationship, and embracing arms (like those of the Great Mother)

and *Set-Apart (Sabbath) Time:* day of rest or holy day, honeymoon, vacation, daily time out (for prayer, ritual, re-creation), time commuting to and from special occasions

and *Quaternities or Four-fold-ness:* baseball diamond, four-petaled flowers (rose, lotus), four rivers of Eden, four points of compass, square, four elements (earth, air, water and fire), four seasons, Grail castle, cross, four humours, four functions, the numbers 4, 40, 44, 400, 4000

ing, digging a well, planting seed/plants, falling asleep, going downstairs (especially into basement), diving into water, going into underworld (the *nekyia* of Odysseus, and also Jesus, Persephone, Dante, etc.)

These are some of the ways the journeying or moving-through-change pattern is expressed in general. The stages of the journey that result in transformation are detailed on pages 18–20.

Some Symbols of These Complements Uniting

THE SACRED MARRIAGE—*Images of Masculine and Feminine or Heaven and Earth joining:*

> King and queen, male and female (wedding, androgyne, hermaphrodite), sun and moon, yin and yang, star of David, seal of Solomon, cross, rainbow, tree, Capricorn and Sagittarius (and Gemini, if brother and sister twins)

and, Images of Completion (which reflect this joining in a less obvious way):

a. *Things which were always there (the static pattern) being discovered or found (the moving pattern):* buried treasure uncovered, Grail (and castle) reached, storage room with old and new things, catch of fish (dragnet thrown into the lake), finding one's home, love or happiness ("lived happily ever after") found, finding hidden island (*King Kong*) or garden (*The Secret Garden*) or valley (*Shangri-La*) or cave with riches (*Aladdin*)

b. *The missing piece which is needed for completion (the static pattern) is found (the moving pattern):* tenth coin, one hundredth sheep (Jesus' examples), missing piece of the puzzle or mystery, piece missing from the collection, last piece of patchwork quilt or garment being fitted into place, the lost chord (or missing word) being found

c. *The place of harmony (static pattern) to which come disparate parts or things or people for rest (moving pattern):* home, the Peaceable Kingdom, the New Jerusalem, "somewhere over the rainbow", Paradise regained, heaven, the kingdom within, wondrous worlds (Oz, Narnia), the interior castle

Some Symbols of the New Creation Born from This Union

The Extraordinary Being or Thing:

a. *That which shines:* saint with halo or aura, divine being with aura or mandorla ("the glory"), golden figure (Buddha), transfigured being (Christ on Mount of Transfiguration), person with subtle or etheric body revealed: an "Easter person" (white garment, numinosity), star ("let your light shine"), stained glass figures with light shining through, objects of gold, shining treasure or gems

b. *Larger-than-life being:* "mana figures," king, queen, emperor, empress, cosmic or primordial man or woman (e.g. Adam or Eve), gods, goddesses, great hero, superhero (Superman, Wonder Woman), miraculous creatures (great fish, magic animals), wise old woman or man

c. *Those who can fly (i.e. get above ordinary life):* angel, winged creatures (fairies, birds), person who can fly

d. *Those used as channels:* the musician, the artist, the interpreter, the medium, the prophet or evangelist, Aquarius, the shaman, the teacher

e. *Resurrected creatures:* Lazarus, the phoenix, butterfly coming out of cocoon, prisoner coming out of jail

f. *Magical child ("become as little children"):* special baby, wondrous youth, homunculus (the "little person" already complete within each of us, shown in many icons)

g. *One who is self-contained, one-unto-one's self:* (psychological) virgin, Virgo

The Journey or Transformation Image, in More Detail

We can chart the stages of the journey—whether it goes out, up, in or down—in these three major segments:

- NORMAL LIFE (which can also include a BIRTH stage, and even PRE-BIRTH)
- DEATH TO THAT LIFE
- NEWER, BETTER LIFE (which comes after the dying)

For Christians, this is known as the Paschal Mystery and Jesus' life exemplifies it fully.

Examples of the Pattern of the Paschal Mystery in Nature:

• sun is in the sky	sun "dies"	sun reborn
• moon is in the sky	moon "dies" (new)	moon reborn
• animal functioning	goes into hibernation	comes back to life
• caterpillar	cocoon (tomb)	butterfly
• earth flourishes (summer, fall)	life "dies" (winter)	earth reborn (spring)
• woman carries baby	pain of labor	new life born
• phoenix (legendary)	thrown into fire	reborn from ashes

Examples of the Pattern of the Paschal Mystery in Fairy Tales and Stories:

• Many heroes' journeys (*Ein Heldenleben*)	trials	changed person
• Sleeping Beauty as girl	deep sleep	awakened to richer life
• Cinderella at ball	changes at midnight	offered life as princess
• Snow White in exile	apple, sleep	offered life as princess
• Peter Rabbit at home	in watering can	back home sadder but wiser
• Pinocchio as puppet	kidnapped, in whale	Pinocchio as real live boy

Examples of the Pattern of the Paschal Mystery in our Lives

• innocence of childhood	shock of school	broader world
• living at home	leave the nest	making it on own
• single life	giving up aloneness	richer life with another
• youthful energy	signs of aging	wisdom of maturity
• lack of suffering	suffering embraced	deepening of spiritual life
• life	death	life after death

"...FOR IT IS IN DYING THAT WE ARE BORN AGAIN" – *PRAYER OF ST. FRANCIS*

From: *Coming Home: A Manual for Spiritual Direction.* Copyright © 1986 by Betsy Caprio and Thomas M. Hedberg, S.D.B. Used by permission.

THE PASCHAL MYSTERY IN SCRIPTURE

	1 NORMAL LIFE	2 "DEATH"	3 NEWER, BETTER LIFE
OLD TESTAMENT:			
• Noah—Gen. 5–9	before the flood	enclosed in ark	after flood, with God's promise
• Joseph—Gen. 37–39	life in Holy Land	thrown in well	high rank in Egypt
• Moses (baby)—Ex. 2	born to Hebrew family	afloat in Nile	rescued by princess
• Israelites—Exodus	slaves in Egypt	wander in desert	return to Promised Land
• Jews—Isaiah	lived in homeland	exile in Babylon	return to Promised Land
• 3 Young Men—Daniel 3	persecuted for religion	in fiery furnace	allowed to worship freely
• Jonah—Jonah	fleeing from his mission	in sea, then fish	back on land, serves God
NEW TESTAMENT:			
• JESUS—Gospels	33 years on earth	death, entombment	Resurrection, glorified
Infancy—Mt. 2	birth, babyhood	flight into Egypt	return to Promised Land
• Parables: —yeast—Mt. 13:33–35	yeast and flour separate	yeast buried	bread rises, yeast leavens
—prodigal son—Lk. 15:11–32	wandering	worse than pigs	returns home
—wheat, grain—Jn. 12:24–25	just a seed	planted (buried)	wheat grows
—pearl, treasure—Mt. 13:44–46	hidden from view	person sells all	person rich, owns the best
• Peter—Gospels	follows Jesus, questions	denies Jesus	great fervor, leads Church
• Paul—Acts 9	persecutes Christians	zapped	great fervor, preaches
BIBLE AS A WHOLE:			
• Humankind	1. the garden, paradise	expelled from garden	new paradise: kingdom of God
	2. centered on self	conversion, death to the old life	centered on God, "born again", "new creation"
• the sacred place	Jerusalem (esp., temple)	Jerusalem destroyed	New Jerusalem, the Holy City

OTHER EXAMPLES OF THE SAME PATTERN

	1 NORMAL LIFE	2 "DEATH"	3 NEWER, BETTER LIFE
• the liturgical year	Advent-Christmas-Epiphany	Lent, esp. Holy Week	Easter and Pentecost time
• the Mass	person away from altar	gives self away (Offertory)	person united with Christ
bread	wheat	ground in mill	bread
wine	grapes	crushed in press	wine
• Baptism	not yet initiated	descends into water	new person (white garment)
• Holy Saturday service (Easter Vigil)	church without fire	plunged into darkness	Easter candle, new light
• Alchemy	*prima materia*	"cooked"	philosopher's stone or *lapis*
• Oxherding pictures of Zen Buddhism	finding bull	merging into no-thing	back in the world

"THOU ART THE JOURNEY
AND THE JOURNEY'S END..."
— ALFRED, 9TH CENTURY SAXON KING

Some Sample Handouts

The pages that follow can be copied and given to those in direction (if they do not have a copy of this book) at the appropriate time—and knowing when that time is for each piece of information is, again, part of the art of spiritual direction. One way we have found useful is to have a folder for each person who comes to do the inner work. In it goes one copy of everything we have to share. Before a visit from anyone, a flip through their folder will show what they have not yet received in the way of handouts; this refreshes the guide's memory so that when the occasion arises he or she can have "just the right thing" at hand. Striking the balance between overwhelming directees with too much material, and not giving them all the help possible to support their journey, is part of the art.

The last six pages were designed as reflection sheets (with two sides) for inquirers and catechumens in the Rite of Christian Initiation of Adults in a parish. Later, it became clear that they were also appropriate for use with people in direction. Al-though the latter group may be expected to be somewhat more at home with spiritual matters, we have found that many people have never answered the basic questions of adult conversion for themselves: "Who is God?" "Why do I belong to this church?" "How do I see Jesus?" and—most basic of all—"What am I doing here?" (Those using this book who are not Christians can make the necessary adaptations to their own faith.)

There are many ways to function as spiritual companion for others; one of the most helpful ways is when we are teacher. The handouts that follow are aids that enable us to do that; the reader will want to develop his or her own special handouts, of course, and find other sources of synthesized material. (Two of the best sources are the leaflets from Dove Publications and the "Catholic Update" series from St. Anthony Messenger Press.)[19] Remember though—many people won't read what is given to them!

A Letter to One Beginning Direction

Dear

I am happy that we are going to be sharing a part of your inner journey for a while, and have found it helpful to sum up in advance a little of my thinking about this sort of relationship.

Companions and guides for the search come in different flavors. My own way of viewing this ministry is as a mirror-holder—someone with whom you explore the things that are happening inwardly and outwardly, and who then helps you step back and take a look at what's happening. We are so close to our own lives that it's hard to be objective about them, isn't it? But, when we tell our stories, and someone else hears them and then sees links between the pieces, we gain an objectivity and a perspective. We see more clearly how God is working in our lives.

The ability to reflect back, and the eyes and ears to see the forest as well as the trees, comes much more from within the seeker than from the companion. Most important of all, there is a third partner in our relationship: the God of truth and freedom and new life, who has been calling you since time began. Let's pray, together, that our hours together honor that call and its Sender.

Lately, this story has been speaking strongly to me about spiritual growth. It is an Hasidic tale:

> Rabbi Susya was very ill, and at his advanced age it was clear that he would not live much longer. He was very sad, and told a friend about his approaching death in gloomy tones. The friend said, "Well, are you afraid God will think you didn't turn out like Moses?" The rabbi replied, "Oh no, I'm afraid God will think I didn't turn out like Susya."

ONE OF A KIND

May we, together, continue uncovering the unique person God has called you to become—it is like no one else who has ever been or will be!

I find it most helpful if people faithfully log their dreams and work in their journals between visits, and then do some summing up to prepare for our all-too-short hour. (A few suggestions on ways to prepare are enclosed.) Every six months or so, it's really useful to step back and take a pulse-reading to see how both of us feel about the relationship between us, *and its fruits*. This way, we have some built-in evaluation, and can then consider whether or not to continue.

A typical session might include five minutes or so of catching up on the "what's happening?" sort of news, then some brief prayer time and a half-hour or so on the one most important thing that has been sent to you for enlightenment since our last visit—it might be a dream that we go over in depth, or some active imagination you have done, or an outer event, or further exploration of a favorite story on which you are working, or some fruit or difficulty in your prayer life. You may prefer to use this largest chunk of time to make a sand tray. We would close with prayer. How does this sound to you?

Thank you for the privilege of sharing in your coming home to our God.

Let's pray for each other,

To Make the Most of Your Visits

Regularly record in your journal:

1. inner events—dreams (and reflections on them—see handout), fantasies; projections recognized, prayer and meditation experiences, feelings, questions, etc., etc., etc.

2. outer events that are important—special Scripture messages, encounters with people, special pictures/movies/t.v. shows, songs, etc., important events, synchronistic events

All of these are clues sent from God to call you to wholeness, to point to next steps in your spiritual growth. They are a form of revelation (small ''r''), or manifestations of God's presence in your life at this time . . . our task is to keep our antennae out for these signs, then ask questions like ''Why is this happening in my life at this time?'' and ''What is the spiritual meaning of this happening?''

spiritual seeker with antennae out for clues to growth

Before coming:

1. Look over your journal entries for connecting threads— or themes—or images—or patterns.

2. Look over our handout on ''Some Basic Questions . . . '' to see if there's one area or one question that speaks strongly to you.

3. Prioritize what you'd like to use our hour for— of the ten different important things that have happened spiritually, which is most important? Which second in importance? (This discipline is really helpful . . . and the things that we don't get to will often attach themselves to what we do focus on . . . or they will move to top priority for the next visit.)

After a visit:

1. Record the major things that seemed to happen.

2. Spend some time on any ''homework''—further mulling over an important dream that has not yet given up its meaning, drawing it, other active imagination steps, etc.

Spiritual Direction
Background Information Form

(Please fill in as much as you can share comfortably—it's all confidential, of course)

Name _____

Address _____

Birthday and place of birth _____

Referred by _____

Date of first visit _____ Phone _____

YOUR INNER LIFE

Are you a practicing member of any religious body? If so, which? _____
How long? _____

What is the extent of your reading/study of C.G. Jung's thought? _____
_____

When did you begin? _____

How much time do you give (on the average) to your inner life (prayer, journal-keeping, active imagination, study, dream logging, etc.)? _____ hours per day.

How would you characterize the *quality* of this time? (e.g. "I'm at my best" or "dregs"!)
_____

Do you foresee having to cut anything out of your schedule to make time for the inner exploring? If so, what will go? _____
_____

Do you keep a journal? _____ with words only—or pictures too? _____

Do you log your dreams? _____ for how long have you done this? _____

Do you record all dream fragments, or just key dreams? _____

How do you usually work with important dream material? _____
_____

Have you ever had a typology evaluation (Myers-Briggs, other?)_____

24

What were the results?_____Do you have your natal (birth) chart available?_____

What is your previous experience with spiritual direction? counseling or therapy?

_____

_____

_____

Have you had some initial dream that seems to be connected to your first visit here—or, perhaps, an important outer event or "marker", or even an outer synchronistic event that might be related to our visit?_____

_____

_____

_____

(use extra paper if necessary)

YOUR OUTER LIFE

I am __single __married __divorced __separated __widowed __ordained minister
__religious

My children are (please list ages too): _____

_____

_____

Are both of your parents living? _____

   If either is living, where? _____

"It is the quality of one's relationship to God that determines one's relationship to all else—other people, work/ministry, all of Creation . . ."

WHEREVER YOUR TREASURE LIES,
♥ THERE WILL YOU FIND YOUR HEART...
— MATTHEW 6:21

Please list the children of your parents, including yourself, with ages and present place of residence for each: _____

_____

_____

_____

What sort of ministry are you involved in at present? _____

_____

_____

_____

and in the past? _____

_____

_____

_____

and what new areas of ministry might be on the horizon for you? _____

_____

_____

_____

There may be other things in your life you would like to share that will help me to get a fuller picture of you— pertinent medical history, a sense of your religious history, information about your religious community (if you belong to one), dreams (waking or sleeping), spiritual goals—or fantasies! You could write about these on a second sheet of paper, or come prepared to share them at our first visit. We will talk about *your expectations* in spiritual direction at that time, as well as mine.

"IF YOU SEEK ME,
YOU WILL FIND ME"

— DEUTERONOMY 4:29

6 Steps for Honoring Your Dreams

1. Record the dream: Write down all the details, feelings and fine points of each dream. Dating them is helpful.

2. Write down any associations you have for anything in the dream: What connections or memories do the people or things or places in the dream have for you? (for example: a dream of my grandparents' home might stir up memories of peace and security and love–or it might have completely different associations.)

Perhaps the dream seems to parallel some story you know (for example: a dream about being sent out into unknown territory might remind you of stories as different as those of Abraham or the voyages of the Starship *Enterprise*.)

There are books of symbols that can give you background about how people of all times and places have used various images which may occur in dreams. (e.g. *Dictionary of Symbols* by Cirlot)

3. Do something with the dream—Draw it, or write a dialogue with one of the characters or symbols from the dream, or use a picture (drawn or mental) of something from the dream as a prayer-starter.

This will help unlock the meaning of the dream.

4. Listen to the dream as if it were a play or a movie or scripture story: If I saw this on the stage or in a theatre, what would it be about? Can you state the *theme* of the dream in a sentence?

Viewing a dream objectively in this way often helps it to release its meaning.

5. Try to discern what the message of the dream is: Dreams have a purpose; they inform us about things we aren't conscious of in waking life. (This is called the *compensatory* function of the dream.)

What does the unconscious/what does God want me to become conscious of through this dream? You will know you have it right when there is a feeling of sureness, a "click".

6. Response: What action can I take to respond to the dream message or teaching? If we do something in response to a dream, we will often experience a release of energy; the dream shows us another step in the process of spiritual growth.

Throughout the process, prayer and sharing with one's spiritual guide help greatly.

Journal-Keeping: A Special Aid to Spiritual Growth

Everyone will develop his or her unique style of journal-keeping . . . so here are just a few suggestions. Please experiment until you find what's best for you.

Suggestion #1: Use something for a journal that does honor and respect to its contents–that is, to your soul and its growth. What we use as a journal says something about how much we value the soul.

Suggestion #2: Be creative. . . . since there are no rules as to what can go in your journal, experiment with many sorts of things, such as:

- records of important events in your life
- favorite quotes or sayings or lines from songs
- Scripture passages that suddenly catch you up
- important dreams (you may find you need a more informal dream log by your bed for recording dreams)
- pictures that illustrate your dreams
- other drawings or pictures you have cut out
- questions
- answers
- memories that resurface and need to be tended to
- personal symbols: images that speak to you and your associations and amplifications for them, plus active imagination with them in one of several forms (e.g. dialogue, drawing, etc.)
- feelings that surface, and some notes about the triggers to those feelings if you know them. . . .

also some "fleshing out" of the feeling (what does it look like? say?)

- summaries and reviews of segments of your life. Time lines are helpful here, as are time lines with projections for the future (always write these in pencil!)
- "coincidences": those synchronistic things that happen "by accident."
- prayers, conversations with God

and much, much more

Suggestion #3: Read some of the famous journals of history and see how helpful the process of journal-keeping was to the writer as he or she developed. Some of these are:

> *Confessions*–Augustine
> *Journal of a Soul*–Pope John XXIII
> *Markings*–Dag Hammarskjöld
> *Memories, Dreams, Reflections*–C.G. Jung
> *Gift From the Sea*–Anne Morrow Lindbergh
> *Autobiography*–Teresa of Avila
> *Autobiography*–Thérèse of Lisieux
> *The Sign of Jonas*–Thomas Merton
> *Diary*–Anne Frank

and many more.

Active Imagination

O.K. I've met this inner witch (critic, brat, etc.) in my dreams and/or in projected form—now, what do I do with it?

We-l-l-l-l—just what you'd do with an outer person or animal or, even, object (or feeling or mood) you need to be in relationship with. . . . Get to know 'em, listen to 'em, befriend them, care for them.

Here are some of the ways you can do that:

Dialogue (in your journal or on tape, or in your imagination)–get in a calmed state and hold a conversation with the person (or object), allowing the feelings and thoughts of him/her/it to bubble up from within. For example:

Me–"Well, you old witch, you certainly don't act very well–why do you shriek and howl like that?"

W–"It's the only way I can get your attention."

Me–"Oh. Well–you've got it. What do you want to tell me about yourself?"

W–"I'm mad. . . ."

and so on. The inner voice will have surprising things to say–just put them down *without* editing.

Acting Out. Is there some place you could allow the inner character to be expressed? An enemy soldier (or army) in your dreams could, perhaps, be taken to the tennis court or gym or aerobics class, and given a workout. An inner critic could read a book with you, or watch a t.v. program, or get on top of local or national politics–and be asked his or her opinion.

Chances to dress up and *really* act the part are great!–can you be a Hallowe'en witch? a clown of some kind? Could you dance/move as the inner person(s) might?

Art as a way of getting the inner figure *out there*–so it can be seen and related to. You can draw, paint, sculpt in clay, make sand pictures, collage. At the very least, a picture can be sketched of the image and put where you will see it often. Just live with it, let it speak to you (Jung's "carry it in your pocket"). Or, find a special place/chair/spot for it/him/her to stay

Important figures/animals/objects from within can have special journal sections–or even an entire book to themselves, in which we

- flesh out a description of them, with pictures (how they act, look; their name)

- work up their biographies: what are the roots of this person/thing in us?

- record the times he/she/it manifests itself/himself/herself. How does it act in me?

  This can be an ongoing record–*and we will note how the inner figure changes.*

- put other incarnations of the same archetypal figure, from stories, Scripture, movies, t.v., etc. (amplification)

- record dialogues with the inner figure, especially about his/her/its feelings and ours–and the limitations we must impose on this part of ourselves (e.g. "O.k., Inner Critic, I know you see everything wrong with how I cleaned the house–but I don't want to hear it.")

- delight in the plusses this character inside has brought to our nature and thank it for this

- accept the minuses it/he/she has brought us

- record prayer for and about this part of ourselves

The Goal: *To make the inner figure conscious. . . .* and help it *stay* conscious. If we neglect an important part of ourselves that has surfaced to consciousness once, it often repeats its unconscious behavior and we have to start over again to get to know it/her/him (I thought I dealt with you last year"—"You did, but then you neglected me, so here I am again! Surprise!")—but it's never as long a process the second (or tenth) time around as it was the first time—it's like renewing an old acquaintance.

Some Basic Questions About Spirituality

- What sort of person would you like to be 5 years from now? 10? On your deathbed, what would you like to have come to?

- If you were asked to describe your spiritual path—or "rule of life"—how would you do that? How have you come to it?

- Do you have a map of spiritual growth—that is, a sense of where there is to go spiritually, and how to get there . . . along with some idea of the milestones or checkpoints or benchmarks along the way? How has the paschal mystery—old life that dies and new life that is born—been lived out in your life?

- How would you picture the soul or the psyche?

- What do you think is the biggest gap in your spiritual life now? It might be the need to add something. Or might it be an incompleteness over some vital moral decision? Or it might be the need for healing and/or finishing unfinished business. Or it might be a needed change of attitude or behavior. Which Scriptural admonitions are most difficult for you?

- Do you have a sense of your personal story or life in overview? What is it God is calling you to at this time? Does your life have a theme? If someone wrote your biography, what would be a good title for it? What are your goals for the years that remain— spiritual goals, others too? Are there Scriptural parallels?

- How do you feel about the fruits your life is bearing . . . in all its areas? Are the pieces of your life (family, community, other relationships, work, time for yourself, etc.) coming together? Are you creating something beautiful for God? What are your special gifts—and are they being used?

  C.G. Jung wrote (about the individuating person) that s/he "must bring forth values which are an equivalent substitute for (his or her) absence in the collective . . ." (The Symbolic Life).

- If you think about your relationship to God over the years, can you trace its development? How has your image of God changed? How has your prayer (kinds of prayer, times for prayer, fruits of prayer) developed? Who is Jesus for you now? earlier?

- Write up a list of the ingredients of your spiritual life—in the past, in the present and for the future. Which practices were once important, but have been dropped—or did they slip away unnoticed? Is that o.k.—or are there things lost in need of finding? Which of the ingredients do you see as essentials for yourself? Which are optionals? Have your ideas on what is essential changed over the years? Where might the emphases shift in the future?

- Do you still have attacks of "C.G." (Christian Guilt) over taking time for your spiritual growth and the inner work it requires? Here's a spine-stiffener: "No one can know God who has not first known him/herself" (Meister Eckhart). On a scale with leaving spiritual growth all to God (Quietism) at one end—and thinking you can make the sanctity happen by working at it tooth and nail (Pelagianism) where would you place yourself at this time? Is this a change from where you once were?

- Do you think these questions will keep us busy for a while?

The Container or Enclosure—
An Important Jungian Concept

TEMENOS: Greek for "sacred precinct"

A set-apart space (like a sacred grove of trees, or the area around a temple) which was dedicated to a god.

C.G. Jung writes (in *Psychology and Alchemy,* Vol. 12 of the Collected Works)

"The drawing of a . . . circle is an ancient device used by everyone who has a special purpose in mind. He thereby protects himself from the "perils of the soul" . . . This same procedure has also been used since olden times to set a place apart as holy and inviolable; in founding a city, for instance, they first drew the . . . original furrow."

—paragraph 63

We are familiar with the concept of bounded space, or the *temenos,* in present-day religion as well. Our churches and temples and synagogues are sacred enclosures. Within them, we have other sacred set-apart spaces: sanctuaries, chancels, tabernacles, the holy of holies . . .

and Scripture is full of such images:

- the paradisaical garden

- Noah's ark

- the ark of the Covenant

- the temple in Jerusalem

- Jerusalem itself

- Jesus' set-apart space of prayer

- the holy city of Revelation

- the promised land

All of these are outer expressions of an inner reality: the sacred space we call the soul—often pictured as a mandala.

The Container Concept in Spiritual Direction

In this ministry there are several ways we can use the concept of boundedness or enclosure . . . in Jungian circles it is made much of and considered very helpful, because we are then echoing in *visible* form that which is *invisible*—the soul or the psyche. For instance, sand tray expert Dora Kalff says:

> "When the psyche is given a free and sheltered space it naturally tends to wholeness . . ."

She is speaking of the box used in Sandplay. It has boundaries, is a sheltered space—yet within it, the person using it has complete freedom. This safe place "looks like" the invisible soul of persons, and so helps them express their soul images, thereby making them more conscious.

Some examples:

- our place of meeting, which (ideally) is a safe "nest"

- the journal and/or dream log someone keeps, which tells the story of his or her soul

- the limits of time we put on our sessions: they help the psyche become used to another boundary

- beginnings and endings of our sessions—a regular format also provides enclosure (prayer, hug, etc.)

- contained space in which someone does art work (the drawing paper) or depicts his/her life in miniature (the sand tray)

- the relationship between guide and 'guidee': if it is known to be safe (that is, strictly confidential) then it becomes freeing

- even a favorite story (a picture of me) may have a stock opening and ending—"Once upon a time . . . lived happily ever after."

- the religious group or church to which we belong, with all its tradition and history

- the trip to and from our meeting place—time that acts like parentheses

In each of these, there is a sense of containment, of holding within-ness. According to Jung and his followers, this is an invaluable aid in triggering the completeness and containment that is natural to the psyche—but may not yet have been revealed to the person. It is especially helpful for someone to have this sense in times of stress. Then, we long for set-apartness; we say things like "I want to go home . . ."

I might ask myself:

- do I have several ways of bounding my spiritual life at this time?

- are there ways other than the ones mentioned above? what could I add to this list?

- if this is a concept not very well lived out in my life just now, where might I begin to add some sense of sacred space?

the ultimate temenos

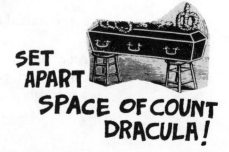

SET APART SPACE OF COUNT DRACULA!

Stories: Pictures of the Soul

MYTHS & LEGENDS

SCRIPTURE

MOVIES

NOVELS

ROMANCES

STORIES

FABLES

T.V. STORIES

DRAMA

SCIENCE FICTION

FAIRY TALES

COMIC STRIPS

MYSTERIES

PARABLES

A story can be understood in the same way as a dream–that is, as a carrier of knowledge about the soul. However, it has a beginning, an unfolding of plot, and an ending. A story we are drawn to speaks of *change* within the soul.

The reason a story is a favorite is because it corresponds to something that's going on–or that needs to go on–within us. The story that grabs us is a hook for our projections of something inside that is asking to be made more conscious. When we learn how to understand the correspondence between inner and outer story, we have a valuable tool for self-knowledge and increased consciousness.

TWO BASIC WAYS TO VIEW A STORY
(cf. 2 ways to explore a dream)
1. *Only as inner–*
   (Intrapersonal)
Everything in the story is something *within* the person it depicts. For example, in the fairy tale *Rapunzel*, the young girl in the tower, the sorceress who locks her up, the prince, her parents, and even the tower and the rampion (or lettuce) her mother longs for are seen as ingredients of one psyche.
   The events of the story depict a drama of transformation going on within one personality.

2. *Inner & outer*
   (Both intrapersonal and interpersonal)
We *identify* with one of the characters in the story (e.g. Captain Ahab, Saint Barbara, St. Peter, Jesus, Red Riding Hood, etc.) The other components of the story may be either within us or without (or both).

This method, the more common, has been used by Ignatius in the Spiritual Exercises, by Lyman Coleman and others in their relational Bible study, by Eric Berne for his T.A. Life Scripts, and by many others.

5 STEPS FOR UNLOCKING A FAVORITE STORY

(an intrapsychic approach, the first of the two ways cited above, based primarily on the style of Dr. Meredith Mitchell of Los Angeles and also the work of Dr. Marie-Louise von Franz.)

Stories that have come to us through oral tradition–RELIGIOUS STORIES, MYTHS and FAIRY TALES–tell especially about transformation within a personality.

Step 1: Record the story *as remembered*. What in the story draws or repels you to/from it?

Step 2: The Title. This tells the most important thing activated in the personality at this time,

33

and/or summarizes the message of the story. Associate and amplify (with research) the images of the title, then try to boil down into psychospiritual language (e.g. *The Golden Bird* =s *a most precious flight of spirit*)

GOLDEN

BIRD

Step 3: Overview of the Story. Look at the story as a whole. Usually, it will be in four parts, about movement from one inner condition [at the beginning] to something more developed [at the end]. (Some stories, however, are about regression, or standing still)

INITIAL CONDITION, SETTING *(who, when, what, how?)*	EXPOSITION, or DEVELOPMENT OF PLOT, "PERIPETEIA" (longest)	CLIMAX or CULMINATION	ENDING or LYSIS: FINAL CONDITION or OUTCOME
A picture of the soul as it is now: what's missing that needs redemption? or what is the conflict/imbalance that needs to be resolved? what is the problem?	The ups and downs, which aid or impede the transformation process. What triggers the action?	The height of the tension. Something happens or changes, giving insight into what has come before.	Result(s): more conscious, stable? less? no change? How does the change affect the life in this personality?

This can lead to the general statement:
"In the personality illustrated by this story, an initial imbalance of _____ leads to a transformation process (or redemption) resulting in the illustrated final condition, which is _____."

Therefore, someone attracted to this story has something similar going on inside. . . . and the details of how the change or transformation is made *in the story* can help one discover how to do the same in his/her life . . . thereby taking more responsibility for it.

Step 4: Work through the story, keeping a consistent attitude, at 3 levels:

- *The Images*—how does each contribute to the outcome (or impede it)? What are my associations for people, animals, things, events (just as for dreams)?

- *Their Meaning in the Psyche*—What in me feels/acts like that? (each thing in the story stands for something in the psyche and acts in accordance with its own principle or purpose.) Keep in context of how the image acts in *this* story.

- *What That Means in Our Life*—How does this archetype or component of the psyche manifest itself or behave or express its nature? (e.g. "Here is how someone might experience this in their life/behavior. . . .", "This is what it might be like to take a bite of a poison apple, or _____") No judgments!

Step 5: Using this knowledge (which is the whole point, just as with a dream!):

- In what way is this story—and my understanding of it—about my life?

- Where am I in this story—at the beginning? in the middle? at the ending?

- How can I use what I've learned to bring about the same transformation in my life?

- How can I live out the new, changed life that develops at the end of this tale's process?

- What story is next?—or is this one a "life myth", spanning several sub-stories? (We know we have lived through to the end of a story when it has lost its power to fascinate.)

- How can I keep this story before me, so its gift of consciousness doesn't slip back into unconsciousness? How can I honor it, pay it some homage for what it has taught me?

- How can I thank God for it?

FAIRY TALES. . . . A BIBLIOGRAPHY

I. BASIC COLLECTIONS OF FAIRY TALES
(gathered from oral tradition)

- *The Grimm Brothers' Fairy Tales (found in many versions)*
  The nursery tales of Germany, first published in 1812. There are over 200 in the collection, and it is useful to find an edition with the standard numbering (e.g. *Rapunzel* is Grimm #12), as different editions give different names for many of the tales.

- *Hans Christian Andersen's Fairy Tales*
  A curious hybrid of folk tale and created story by the gifted Danish 'dream weaver,' the first of which were published in 1835. Based on the stories of the folk, many of these have been assimilated *into* oral tradition. There are over 150 Andersen tales.

- *The Arabian Nights' Entertainment (or, The Thousand and One Nights)*
  These are the chronicles of the ancient kings of Persia, whose empire extended into Arabia, India, Egypt, Palestine and as far east as China. First translated from Arabic into French in 1704. These are *long* stories.

- *French Fairy Tales*
  The French began collecting and editing their folk tales early on, the two best known collections being those of Countess D'Aulnoy of 1682 and Charles Perrault of 1697. Many are paralleled by the Grimms' tales.

- *The Classic Fairy Tales* by Iona and Peter Opie. (London: Oxford Univ. Press, 1974)
  A superb book giving the first English translation of 24 best-loved tales. Of special importance is the historical background of each story, and an overall survey of how the collecting of these folk tales began. Available in paperback, but the hardcover version has wonderful colored pictures.

- *The Andrew Lang Fairy Books*–12, available in paperback from Dover Publications, 31 East 2nd St., Mineola, NY 11501 (send for their juvenile book catalog)
  In 1889, *The Blue Fairy Book* by English folklorist Lang appeared. Over the years at the turn of the century it was followed by eleven other "colors" of fairy tales: *Red, Yellow, Green, Grey, Lilac, Olive, Orange, Pink, Brown, Crimson* and *Violet.* They are the most complete collection of fairy tales from all around the world, but without an index.

Plus: collections of the folktales from countries east and west, which are readily available. Notable collections have been made, especially, of Celtic and Irish fairy tales, Norwegian fairy tales (*East of the Sun & West of the Moon*), American Indian fairy tales, Japanese fairy tales, Russian fairy tales.

Related Collections of Stories: (which come under the heading of folklore, but are not considered fairy tales)

- Fables–La Fontaine, Aesop

- Parables–those of Jesus, those of other religious traditions (notably the Muslim Sufis and the Jewish Hasidim)

- Myths–the definition of a myth is that it includes some divine intervention

- Legends–legends are based on historical *fact* (e.g., *The Iliad* and *The Odyssey* sprang from the Trojan War). Legends are usually long and contain many sub-plots (e.g. the Arthurian legends, the Welsh *Mabinogian*, the Finnish *Kalevala*, the Norwegian Peer Gynt tales, the Ring of the Nibelung tales of Germany, Robin Hood tales). All religions also have their own legendry, stories that are "truer-

than-true" that have built up around the founders and the saints (e.g. in Christian tradition, the legend of St. Martin of Tours dividing his cloak, of Jesus and Mary and the cherry tree, etc. The medieval *The Golden Legend* by Jacob de Vorignes is a collection of saints' tales).

Also, *composed stories* which are folklore-like, but *not* from oral tradition:

- Romances: composed tales of chivalry from the middle ages and later (e.g. the *Roman de la Rose* of France, 13th century)

- Children's stories of our time: dating back to the 19th century, when the idea began to dawn that childhood was a time to be seen as distinct and precious—not just a diminutive version of adulthood. Many examples: *Alice in Wonderland, Gulliver's Travels, Pinocchio*, George MacDonald and Frances Hodgson Burnett's stories, Frank Baum's OZ series, C.S. Lewis' Narnia stories (several have adult levels too)

- Adult stories of our time: science-fiction, particularly, and also some movies and television series that have become part of our collective mind-set—*Star Trek, E.T., Gone With the Wind* (first in book, then in film version), Sherlock Holmes' stories, many others.

II. WRITINGS ABOUT THE MEANING OF FAIRY TALES:

- Books by Marie-Louise von Franz:
  The Interpretation of Fairy Tales
  Shadow and Evil in Fairy Tales
  The Feminine in Fairy Tales
  Individuation in Fairy Tales
  Redemption Motifs in Fairy Tales
  (Spring Publ., Dallas)
  Dr. von Franz was one of C.G. Jung's closest and most brilliant associates, who began work with him when in her teens and has devoted her

life to continuing what he began. Her books are transcriptions of her lectures at the Jung Institute in Küsnacht, Switzerland, and not organized as clearly as one might hope, but filled with rich information. She uses approach #2 on our flyer—seeing fairy tales as both inner and interpersonal.

- *The Uses of Enchantment*, Bruno Bettelheim (New York: Vintage Books, 1977)
  A renowned Freudian, Dr. Bettelheim's gift to us in this book is the valuing of fairy tales for children (and adults). There is a lack of emphasis on the spiritual that those used to Jungian writers have come to expect.

- *Once Upon a Time*, Max Lüthi (Bloomington, Ind.: Indiana University Press, 1976)
  Especially interesting because written by a folklorist, rather than a psychologist.

- *Fairy Tales and Children*, Carl-Heinz Mallet (New York: Schocken Books, 1984)
  And this one from an educator, an absolutely delightful interpretation of 4 Grimms' tales (*Hansel and Gretel, Little Red Riding-Hood, The Boy Who Set Out to Learn Fear,* and *The Goose Girl*).

- *Fairy Tales: Allegories of the Inner Life*, Jean C. Cooper (Northamptonshire, G.B.: The Aquarian Press, 1983)
  A rich study of the archetypal patterns and symbols in the classic fairy stories.

And what of C.G. Jung himself? Jung touches on fairy tales throughout his collected works, primarily in Volume 9i in the article "The Phenomenology of the Spirit in Fairy Tales" (1948), but this is not an avenue he took off on the way he did with alchemy or the mandala. . . .

But throughout the writings of his followers one can hardly pick up a book without a fairy tale shedding its light. Two writers who especially have mined this vein in print are Ann Ulanov (with her husband Barry) and Linda Leonard (in *The Wounded Woman*). See also James Hillman's work, and Robert Johnson's approach to the Arthurian legends and mythology.

To Summarize! FAIRY TALES are *one* specie of FOLK STORY, which is just *one* category of *FOLKLORE,* which also includes games, customs, art, song, dance, ritual . . . many of which are other ways of telling the fairy tale (e.g. the Child ballads of England, Scotland, and the U.S.)

Projection . . . One of the Best Ways To Learn About Ourselves

Projection is when we give away a part of our soul!

Actually, we (without knowing it) "drape" part of ourselves onto someone else (or something else).

- *What would cause us to do that?*
  Well, the other person has some quality that is very much like a part of ourself we *don't* yet know. That acts as a hook on which we can drape that part of ourself.

- *That sounds terrible . . .*
  No. It's a gift, really—if we can learn from it. When we meet part of ourself we *don't* know, in projected form, it gives us a chance to see that part— then take it back.

- *Well, how do we know we've given away part of ourselves through projection?*
  Good question! It shows up when we have a very strong emotional reaction to someone or something—either a positive or negative reaction.

- *I have strong reactions to a lot of people . . . many people I love dearly, and others I can't stand. Does that mean I'm projecting part of myself onto them?*
  Maybe yes, maybe no (why do you keep asking all these questions?). Some people are very lovable and we love them a lot; others are rotten and we can't bear to be around them. It's an *over*-reaction that indicates more than a usual feeling. That's when we can suspect projection.

- *And this is a good thing?*
  Yes, *if* we understand what's going on. Then we can say, 'What is it about _____that attracts/repels me so? Maybe it's a part of myself I don't know yet.'

- *It's like a clue about ourselves . . .*
  You got it! Projections—and dreams—are about the best way we have of learning about parts of ourselves that are still unconscious.

"I need that part of myself. I'll take it back."

"Great! Now she can really see me as I am."

(This type of projection is technically known as disowning projection.)

(The Other Side of the Story)

- *It sounds as though we all should know about projection and how it works . . . do you think most people do understand?*
  Oh no . . . unfortunately! How could there be so many people angry at each other, or people involved in serial marriages, or Hitler wiping out six million Jews, or . . .

- *Projection causes all that? . . . I'd better understand it so I don't make those mistakes. Let's see now . . . what happens if I project part of myself on someone and I don't know that's happening?*

Well, it sort of looks like this . . .

but before long . . .

- *Then she's still stuck with the unknown part of herself, isn't she?*
  Right. And *unconsciously* she's saying . . .

C.G. Jung wrote:

"I can see no advantage whatever in behaving like an ostrich. It is certainly no ideal for people always to remain childish, to live in a perpetual state of delusion about themselves, foisting everything they dislike onto their neighbours and plaguing them with their prejudices and projections. How many marriages are wrecked . . . because he sees his mother in his wife and she her father in her husband, and neither ever recognizes the other's reality? Life has difficulties enough without that; we might at least spare ourselves the stupidest of them. But, without a fundamental discussion of the situation, it is often simply impossible to break these infantile projections."
—from *The Psychology of the Transference,*
paragraph 420

- *So, when we suspect we are projecting, we need to examine that . . . and spend some time with the projected part of ourselves . . . and recognize it's in us . . . and take it back, or withdraw the projection . . . and keep working to integrate it with the rest of ourselves.*
  We need to own it . . . or, if you like religious language, we need to redeem it.

- *AMEN!*

Projection—Chapter 2
When We Are Projected Upon

"Ha, Ha my pretty . . . Now I'm going to cast a spell upon you . . ."

- *Is it just the person who does the projecting who is the loser?*
  That depends . . . upon whether or not the other person is conscious of receiving a projection or unconscious, and also whether he or she is willing to give it back to the "projector."

  In the fairy tales (which are like collective pictures of what goes on in individual psyches or souls), the person *projected upon* is usually considered to be the one in trouble, not the projector.

- *If I'm unconscious of being the object of projection, I may believe I am the way the other person is seeing me, right?*
  Right—and that can be either as very wonderful (in which case we can get very inflated) or as really awful . . . sometimes both (if a positive projection which isn't lived up to turns negative).

- *So, understanding that it's happening is one safeguard that I don't "fall under the spell". Is that enough?*
  Nope! We have lots of examples all around us of people who know others project on them (as savior, or hero, or goddess, for example) and really solicit that projection.

- *Why would anyone do that?*
  Well, it makes them feel good, usually—maybe their egos are so weak they need to bask in others' good opinion of them. Sometimes we justify putting out a hook for a projection because it gives us control over others—it's a way of manipulating them.

- *As in, "if I can cook just like Joe's dear grandmother, maybe he'll love me more . . . "?*
  Yes—it's a really inauthentic way of living, isn't it? Think what it does to us. Can you see how that's like being caught in a witch's spell?

- *Hmmm . . . I'm getting it. And, from what you've told me before, it's also immoral to solicit part of another person's soul . . . or to keep it once it's given to you.*

"This is getting heavy."

A Quality I Would Like To Say Goodbye To: _____

_____

SOME STEPS THAT HELP

1. Describe in *detail* this quality and how it operates in my life. When does it appear? Are there any triggers that seem to bring it out? Have I always been this way? If not, when did I begin to be this way? What are my best guesses about the *roots* of this way of acting/thinking/being?

2. If I were to personify this quality in myself, what would it look like? What would its name be? How would it dress? What would its favorite expressions be? Can I find a picture of how it looks—or draw one?

3. Dialogue with this inner figure. It needs to hear from me:
   —its good qualities, ways it has helped me and can continue to help me
   —the things it causes me to do that I don't want to continue
   —that I am not who I was; I am now committed to becoming as whole as possible, and so it is time for us to have a confrontation (or two).

   And, imagine a scene of Jesus dialoguing with this inner figure, "taming" it for me.

4. Give it a task to do. If the inner figure I am getting to know is a Critic, for example, how can I put him to work? What *one* area of my life does need the Critic's keen insight (not twenty areas, just one)?

   Can I monitor myself for a while to see if (1) I am using this inner figure for his/her assigned task, and (2) choosing not to allow him/her to take over at other times?

5. What inner character would be the opposite of this one? If I don't know him or her, I need to do steps 1, 2 and 3 with it. This will help to balance the figure that is giving me problems. How can the opposite inner figure be given more time in my daily schedule? What ways can it be brought into reality for me?

6. I need an external measuring stick or touchstone. Is there one regular situation in which this inner figure seems to take over? I need to log myself each time I am in that situation, and assess whether or not the inner figure has had less influence than before—or more—or about the same.

7. This desire to free myself from being controlled by this inner figure needs to be made the subject of prayer—a *primary* intention. Are there three or four other people I can ask to make this a prayer intention as well?

We *can* change. We cannot change by wishing it so, or by willing it so, or by "strength of character". We change when we get to know that within us which is in charge of us—as we get *consciousness* of it, we take away its power to be in charge.

To do this takes time, and a good bit of hard work, and—usually—some pain. Perhaps the pain of living with _____ (whatever) is less than the pain of all this work and self-knowledge. That is our choice.

One Person's Story

"For most of my childhood and all of my adult life I never felt as though I could do things well enough—so I always worked extra hard to do them perfectly. Even then I was never satisfied. There are several factors from my early years that probably contributed to my being this way, one of them being that I was the 'great white hope' of my family, the one who would do well and make everyone else proud.

"I decided this had to change. It was driving me into stress-related illnesses and making my life a constant tension. One day I found this picture! I knew when I saw it that it was a picture of the 'person' inside me that was always expecting me to do better. I heard his name in a dream: Pastor van Voort! (a Puritan, obviously). He says things like 'you must . . . ' and 'you should . . . ' and he also says, 'you can't . . . ' and 'you'll never . . . ' and 'why do you even try?'

"I talked to him. I told him he had to lay off, that it is helpful to have standards and be a hard worker, but that he was too demanding and left no room for other parts of me, like the little girl who likes to play.

"This went on for several months. I wrote out my conversations with him and was surprised to find that he responded. He said he wanted to be in charge of me—and I told him that wasn't going to be possible any more, for I was changing. Things were going to be different. I asked him please to stick around to help me with just one thing, the research I have to do for my work.

"His opposite in me is the kid who likes to goof off and eat ice cream and watch soap operas and horror movies. I found I needed to give her permission to do that, and one day I had her talk to the Pastor. They didn't like each other very much—he doesn't approve of her, and she thinks he's a kill-joy. I asked them to agree to disagree, and to get it straight—finally—that neither of them could be in charge of me.

"I need to keep both their pictures where I can see them. For a touchstone, to see if things were changing, I used my recurring need to prepare even a half-hour class (I'm a teacher) as though I were delivering an entire course. *Gradually* I've seen that I have let go of the need to have that class be perfect—I know I do good work, and when it's ready it's ready. I spend about an hour in preparation for each half hour or 45-minute class now . . . and they're turning out fine. I write this down, so I can see what's happening—that helps.

"One special friend was willing and ready to work with me on this. She promised that she'd pray for me each day, for this special intention—that I would be able to be less of a perfectionist so I could enjoy my life more. I have prayed for that too. It's beginning to feel as though I'm not going to let the Pastor sabotage me forever . . . but it's slow. I hope it's helped you to read about him and me."

"He's a cutie!"

Developing the Functions

C.G. Jung's typology states that we each have four functions. One will be dominant, developed from our early years. Two others will be auxiliary or ancillary. The fourth will be inferior—our connection to the depths of the unconscious.

The question is often asked, "How can I develop my inferior (or another) function?" Here are a few ideas for each of them. For more detail, see the books listed at the end of this handout.

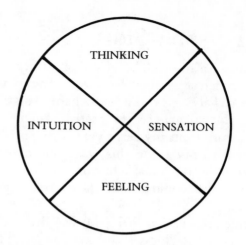

TO DEVELOP SENSATION

EVERYDAY ACTIVITIES	WAYS OF PRAYER
• practice using senses: notice colors, taste food carefully, check out scents and smells, listen to music and sounds around you, pay attention to textures and touch	• use visual and audial aids to prayer: music, pictures, incense, movement, candles, foods, beads
• go on a campaign to help your body function as well (and look as well) as it possibly can	• seek God in nature, all creation
• plant a garden, work with potted plants	• live with the symbols of the sacraments
• start a collection of favorite pictures	• hunt for—and enjoy—the best possible liturgy
• draw, paint, work in sand tray, sculpt	• allow prayer to flow over into works of love for others
• discover your personal symbols—draw them	• find ways to celebrate the liturgical year at home
• find ways to celebrate the natural year (seasons, moon phases)	• revisit the Rosary, other vocal prayer
• be with/observe high sensation people	• the Jesus prayer
• slow down your daily pace: become aware of different actions, stop, look and listen	• be present at Biblical scenes (a la Ignatius); experience with senses
• monitor your intuition (it tends to leap into the future and avoid the now)	• slow down enough to live "sacramentally" (i.e., with the awareness that all life is sacred)
	• bodily prayer (yoga, finding the center, etc.)

To Develop Intuition

EVERYDAY ACTIVITIES	WAYS OF PRAYER
• attend to your dreams, work with them	• practice the presence of God all around you—try to put up reminders of this so you can converse with God all through the day, informally
• try trusting hunches—see what happens	
• be with intuiting people; watch how they function, then try to discover how that quality in yourself feels (they are often the 'leap-froggers')	• block out time to just "be" with God—and see what happens
• use your personal symbols to speak to you—just live with them and let them do their work	• with parables and symbols of scripture imagine Jesus speaking to *you*—what do the stories and images mean?
• enjoy your capacities for fantasy: "What would it be like if _____?"	• imagine how you would be at your most evolved level—and pray for that to become reality
• read science fiction, or fantasy (Narnia, etc.) Imagine yourself there.	• if you had lived in Jesus' time, what would that have been like?
• write a fantastic tale of your own	• all sorts of guided imagery, "you are there" prayer
• monitor sensation in your life; it tends to clutter us with details the senses take in (the need for household order, etc.)	• centering prayer: awareness of God dwelling within carried through the day

To Develop Feeling

EVERYDAY ACTIVITIES	WAYS OF PRAYER

EVERYDAY ACTIVITIES

- count your blessings

- be with feeling people; watch how they function, then try to discover how that quality in yourself feels and acts

- if there are not *some* intimate relationships in your life (people with whom you can share your soul) develop some

- develop your sense of touch and use it in connection with people, appropriately

- monitor the way thinking takes over: not everything has to be analyzed or explained ("the heart has its reasons")

- learn to ask for forgiveness

- if there is no one in your life to love wholeheartedly, find someone or a pet

- allow yourself the luxury of remembering treasured times and people from past

- if without a spiritual friend or companion, search for one

- give of yourself to those in need without expecting anything in return from them

WAYS OF PRAYER

- devotional prayer—messages of love to God

- quiet reflection on Scripture passages about the love of God for us

- intercessory prayer for those in need

- appreciation of Eucharist

- prayer with others, especially healing prayer and prayer with those in pain, crisis

- prayer of thanksgiving for God's gifts

- find a real prayer community or group to pray with regularly

- sing songs of praise and joy

- meditate on the sufferings of Jesus; enter into the Stations of the Cross

- keep alive memories of those who have passed from our life (through death or other circumstances)—pray for them

- make your primary *fear* in life the subject of prayer— watch for changes

TO DEVELOP THINKING

EVERYDAY ACTIVITIES	WAYS OF PRAYER

EVERYDAY ACTIVITIES

- study and build a library
- logging: time, events, activities—anything that helps organize one's mind
- analyze daily situations in life, try to get to bottom of problems
- journal-keeping
- teach something to someone: what will help him or her understand it?
- be with thinking people, watch how they approach things. Can you find that same capacity in yourself?
- monitor the feeling function so it won't dominate thinking—do anger/fear/joy rush to meet each situation so that there's no room for objectivity?
- play thinking games—Scrabble, crossword puzzles, guessing games
- read who-done-its, try to solve the mystery

WAYS OF PRAYER

- Scripture study that leads to prayer
- spiritual reading that leads to prayer
- study of theology that leads to prayer
- discursive (step-by-step) meditation
- try the Breviary or shortened form of the Office
- the prayer of organizing: liturgies, projects, ways of helping the needy, religious education programs (these can be approached as a form of prayer)
- spiritual check-lists, examens, etc. help us organize our soul-life (be sure they're not negative, punitive)
- write down your prayer
- the Ignatian exercises
- trace a theme through Scripture; apply it to your life, pray over it

SOME REFERENCES

Morton Kelsey: TRANSCEND (Crossroad, 1981), pp. 121ff.; CHRISTO-PSYCHOLOGY (Crossroad, 1982) Chapter 7, p. 68ff.

Grant, Thompson and Clarke: FROM IMAGE TO LIKENESS (Paulist, 1983) A very extensive treatment of Jung's typology and Christianity. Excellent list of resources in Appendix A, p. 212

Gordon Lawrence: PEOPLE TYPES AND TIGER STRIPES (Center for Applications of Psychological Type, 1979) Practical thoughts on using our knowledge of typology in education. Also helpful to parents.

Betsy Caprio: THE WOMAN SEALED IN THE TOWER (esp. Appendix) (Paulist, 1983) The functions are correlated with the elements of earth, air, water and fire, with exercises to develop each.

Spiritual Reading Suggestions: Important Teachers in the History of Christian Spirituality

- Jesus and Scripture

I. THE PATRISTIC ERA

- *First Three Centuries:* Clement of Rome, Clement of Alexandria, Cyprian, Ignatius of Antioch

- *Fourth to Seventh Centuries:* Ambrose, Augustine, Cassian, Benedict, Gregory the Great (in the West), Athanasius, Cyril of Jerusalem, Basil, John Chrysostom, Cyril of Alexandria, John Climacus, Antony of Egypt and other desert papas and mamas (in the East)

II. THE MIDDLE AGES

- *The Benedictine School* (focus on monastic life, solitariness as a witness, work and prayer (<u>ora et labore</u>), liturgy
  Anselm, Bernard of Clairvaux, Hildegarde, Gertrude the Great, Mechtilde, Bridget of Sweden, Aelred of Rievaulx

- *The School of St. Victor* (focus on mysticism springing from study of Platonism, associated with Augustinian canons near Paris)
  Hugh of St. Victor, Adam of St. Victor

- *The Dominican School* (focus on balance between contemplative life and action, search for truth— Veritas— takes one many places)
  Dominic, Albert the Great (Albertus Magnus), Thomas Aquinas, Catherine of Siena, Vincent Ferrer

- *The Franciscan School* (focus on simplicity, affective spirituality, poverty)
  Francis of Assisi, Bonaventure, Angela of Foligno, Catherine of Bologna, Jacopone da Todi

- *The German School of Mystics* (based on pseudo-Dionysius and neoplatonism; mostly Dominican)
  Meister Eckhart, John Tauler, Henry Suso, John Ruysbroeck (and nearby, in Flanders), Thomas à Kempis

- *Other Notable Medieval Names:*
  Walter Hilton, Julian of Norwich, anonymous monk-author of *The Cloud of Unknowing,* Lawrence Justinian, Catherine of Genoa, Ramon Lull, Richard Rolle

III. COUNTER-REFORMATION TIMES

- *The Ignatian School* (focus on active, energetic, practical spirituality aimed at forming the will for sanctity and apostolic work)
  Ignatius of Loyola, Robert Bellarmine, many others

- *The Carmelite School* (focus is on the every-thing-ness of God and the corresponding nothingness of humans; aim—complete detachment in order to reach the stage of contemplation)
  Teresa of Avila, John of the Cross

- *The French School:* (pointed the way for the next three centuries, along with Ignatius)
  Francis de Sales, Jane Frances de Chantal, Margaret Mary Alacoque, John Eudes, Louis de Montfort, the "Oratorians" (later, Sulpicians)—Pierre de Bérulle and Jean-Jacques Olier, Vincent de Paul, Brother Lawrence of the Resurrection, Jean-Pierre de Caussade

- *The Protestant Tradition:* Martin Luther, Johann Arndt, John and Charles Wesley, William Law, writings and songs of the Shakers, Quaker writings, Angelus Silesius, Jacob Boehme, the Pietists of the sixteenth century, George Herbert, Emanuel Swedenborg

IV. THE LAST 100 YEARS

- *Europeans:* Charles de Foucauld, Thérèse of Lisieux, Francis Thompson, author of *The Way of the Pilgrim,* Simone Weil, J. H. Newman, C. S. Lewis, Dietrich Bonhoeffer, Nicholas Berdyaev, Pierre Teilhard de Chardin, John Bosco on his dreams, Kahlil Gibran, the monastery at Taizé, France, Friedrich Von Hügel, Abbé Huvelin. (In pre-Vatican II times, the classic text for ascetical theology: Tanquerey's *The Spiritual Life*)

- *Americans* (or U.S. based): (tend to be very practical, also more influenced by contemporary psychologies as aids to spiritual growth)
  Thomas Merton; John Powell, Eugene Kennedy, Henri Nouwen, Adrian van Kaam, William Johnston (marriage of east and west), Matthew Fox, Basil Pennington, Tilden Edwards, Rollo May and Gerald May, authors associated with the House of Affirmation, Louis Savary, Agnes Sanford, Matthew and Dennis Linn and Sheila Fabricant

- *The Jungian School* (has roots in Jung's early followers who bridged his thought with religious thought: e.g. Fr. Victor White, O.P. of England and Jolande Jacobi of Hungary)
  Morton Kelsey, John A. Sanford, Robert Johnson, Ann Ulanov, Ira Progoff, Thomas Clarke, John Welch, Wallace Clift, Elizabeth Howes and Sheila Moon and others associated with the San Francisco Guild for Psychological Studies, authors associated with Pecos Abbey, New Mexico, John Dourley

(Note: Paralleling these Christian authors is a whole body of Jewish spiritual writing: in our time, especially, Martin Buber. The other great religions have their own spiritual writers, all worth exploring: Islam, Taoism, Buddhism, Hinduism. The Yogic literature is another parallel body of work from the east, as is the alchemical tradition in the west. In addition, not to be overlooked, are the primitive religions of the world. Most interesting and enjoying popularity now, the spirituality of native Americans [Indian tribes]).

A suggestion for those exploring Jung-influenced spirituality:

As you read back in the classics of spirituality, which earlier writers/schools are saying things that fit with the Jungian concepts and view of the soul? Much of what C. G. Jung "discovered" was already part of the heritage—but he expressed it in psychological terms, and incorporated it in a complete view of the growth process. Who were his predecessors? (This helps us find our roots.) Which of the authors on this list are coming from a totally *different* viewpoint about the soul and about spirituality than Jung and his Christian interpreters? What are the differences? (This helps us decide which approach to spiritual growth is most natural and comfortable for us.)

The *I Ching* . . . A Growth Tool for Christians?

All the ancient religions had their oracles:

- the Greeks at Delphi and other places

- the Chinese Taoists their "Book of Changes", the *I Ching*

- the Old Testament Jews their Urim and Thummim (see, for example, I Sam. 23:9-12)

Such divination tools died out after the middle ages, as rational thought became the norm . . . but the divination tools remained and usually became debased ("Madame Laura will read the cards for you" and so forth).

However, depth psychologists have tapped back into these unique oracular devices in our time, understanding them from a psychological perspective which explains how they worked . . . even in the years before Christ. The main principle illustrated by the consultation of oracles is PROJECTION; whatever answer we get to the question asked, we use it as a screen upon which to project our already-unconscious awareness of the answer to our question. The oracle acts as a hook to reach down into the unconscious and pull out what is there in our soul. It is a catalyst.

Viewed in this way, the *I Ching* (the most elegant of the ancient oracles) is completely harmonious with Christian thought. There is a woman, in fact, who is writing THE GOSPEL ACCORDING TO THE I CHING as her doctoral (in ministry) thesis! Any dozen Christians could, for example, ask a similar question of the *I Ching* and get the same hexagram as an answer—yet come up with a dozen different ways of applying the very generalized teachings of this famous book. For each it would hook what he or she already knew deep down inside.

But why should we want to consult a Chinese oracle when we have our own Christian ways of growth at hand—and so many of them at that? Can we not consult Scripture for the answer to our questions, or speak of them to God in prayer? Of course, and we do all the time.

Things like the *I Ching* are for extra-special times in our lives. The old rule is, "do all you can to answer your question and only consult any oracular device as a final capstone". For especially important concerns, then, or for the pressing concerns which we seem to get nowhere with on our own, we might consider the *I Ching*. The great *advantage* is that because it is unfamiliar to most Christians, it seems to provide a speedier channel into the unconscious—we don't come to it with the overlay of head-material we bring to Scripture, for instance. The *I Ching* is just another optional tool for self-knowledge.

Also, the *I Ching* is a visual device; it works through right-brain functioning, in images. Most of us are poverty-stricken in our attention to this part of our being . . . a fact we can bemoan—or rejoice in. It is the freshness of this part of ourselves, its undeveloped childlikeness, that makes it so quickly "touchable."

For more on the *I Ching,* see Chapter 9 of John Sanford's *Evil: The Shadow Side of Reality* (New York: Crossroad, 1981).

(N.B. We must always remember that any of the contents of the unconscious—dream, projection, fantasy—need to be subjected to "the light of day," to our good sense. To give them more importance than that is to be engaged in magic, which is something completely foreign to the approach described here.)

YIN   YANG

Using the *I Ching*

Needed: the book of the *I Ching* with directions on how to cast the coins; three coins

Here are suggested steps for Christians who would use this (or any other) oracle:

1. Through prayer, formulate the question you wish to ask. It should not be a "yes" or "no" question, but something for which you would like to find an answer in terms of a pattern or a trend. Typical questions might be:

   • What can I expect as a result of this direction I have chosen?"

   • "If I choose this possible next step, what sort of fruits may come from it—for me and my family?"

   • "How can my learning from this experience be applied?"

   • "What direction does God want me to take in this matter?"

   • How is this specific goal to be accomplished?"

   • "What are my true motives in this situation?" etc.

2. Reflect quietly on the question. Allow it to soak down into you. The answer is already there. God dwelling in your soul knows, and the consultation of the *I Ching* is just a way to release what you need to understand more clearly.

3. With whomever is your companion in your soul's journey, cast the *I Ching* coins or stalks reverentially. Be sure to pray first, asking God to use this unusual tool in a synchronistic way. When the hexagram is finally thrown, accept it openly and let it speak to you. There should be time to reflect on its meaning afterwards.

   A hexagram (and the changed hexagram if one is indicated) should then lead, ideally, to journal work and continued dialogue with the Lord about the question you are exploring.

Here is a chart showing the traditional attributes of each trigram, 2 of which make up one of the 64 hexagrams. (Remember, the hexagram is written from the bottom to the top.)

Play with the images of the 2 trigrams you have thrown, allowing them to seep into you and give you more information about the meaning of the answer to your question. You may want to dialogue with them as you would with a dream symbol. (E.g., "Wind, what does it feel like when you appear over the water, as you have done to me?" Think of all the Scriptural connections you might make for this one.)

TRIGRAM ATTRIBUTES

CH'IEN	HEAVEN SKY DAY	CREATIVE ENERGY STRONG LIGHT	EARLY WINTER COLD ICE	FATHER	ONENESS FIRMNESS	HEAD MIND
K'UN	EARTH NIGHT	WEAK YIELDING DARK NOURISHING	EARLY AUTUMN WARM	MOTHER	ADAPTIVE	BELLY WOMB
CHEN	THUNDER	AROUSING ACTIVE EXCITING	SPRING EARTHQUAKE	ELDEST SON	EXPANSIVE	FOOT
K'AN	WATER MOON	DANGEROUS DIFFICULT ABYSSMAL	MID WINTER CLOUDY	MIDDLE SON	ANXIOUS MELANCHOLY	EAR
KEN	MOUNTAIN	KEEPING STILL IMMOVABLE PERVERSE	LATE WINTER STILLNESS	YOUNGEST SON	CALM STUBBORN	HAND
SUN	WIND WOOD	GENTLE PENETRATING GRADUAL	EARLY SUMMER MILD MOVEMENT	ELDEST DAUGHTER	GENTLE	THIGH
LI	FIRE SUN	CONSCIOUS DEPENDING	MID SUMMER LIGHTNING	MIDDLE DAUGHTER	INTELLIGENT DEPENDENT	EYE
TUI	LAKE	JOYFUL SATISFIED FULNESS PLEASURE	LATE AUTUMN RAIN	YOUNGEST DAUGHTER	OPENNESS EXCESS	MOUTH

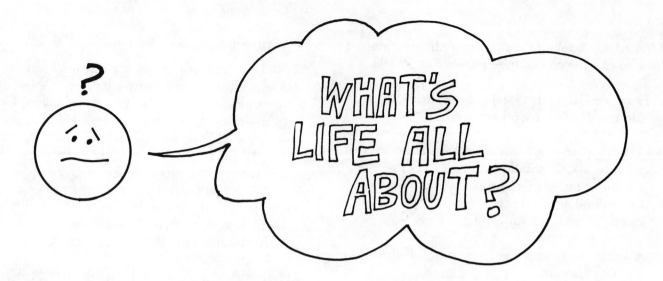

This question is sometimes worded *WHAT IS THE MEANING OF LIFE? WHAT AM I DOING HERE?* or *WHAT ARE PEOPLE FOR?* or even *IS THIS ALL THERE IS?* What Is My Answer to This Question?

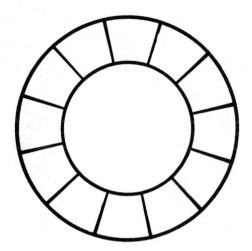

- If this wheel represents my life

- And these are some of the ingredients of my life
  work   family   God   learning
  play   friends   food   sleep

- Which of the ingredients (or others I would add) would go in the *center* of this picture of my life *as it is now*?

  (write it in the center)

- Put the other ingredients of life as it is now in the outside portions of the wheel. Add other things that are important to daily living in the other spaces.

- Am I satisfied with this arrangement of my life's pieces? or would I prefer a change? What might go in the center if I did change things around?

"SEEK FIRST THE KINGDOM OF GOD — AND ALL ELSE WILL BE GIVEN YOU."

– Matthew 6:33

19 _ _ _____

My Journey

1. We are each here on earth for a span of years. On the time line above, please mark:

   - year of birth (yes, you can cheat!)
   - this year (put it at the approximate place in your life: half-way, one third . . .)

   Then would you record:

   - (above the line) the major *external* or *outer* events of your life. You can put them at approximately the time they occurred.
   - (below the line) the major *internal* or *inner* events of your life, also at the time they took place.

2. Now in the part of the time line that you have *not yet lived* (that is, from the present year till the end of the road), will you write in:

   - (above the line) some of your *external* or *outer* goals for the rest of your life (for example: own a home, have a baby, lose 35 pounds, etc.)

   - (below the line) some of your *internal* or *inner* goals for the rest of your life (for example: set aside time for prayer, do more reading, etc.)

3. Finally, can you pretend that you have reached the end of your life?
   Look back on it, reflect on it—and star the things (past and future) you are *most* happy to have accomplished in your time here on earth.

How Do I See God?

As we grow, our image of God changes. On the time line below, can you write in the sort of God you pictured at different stages of your life?

childhood	teen years	young adult years	adult years

Here are some ways people have seen God throughout history. Do any of these fit on your time line?

JUDGE, RECORD KEEPER

ARTIST

STILL, SMALL VOICE WITHIN

SPARK OF LIGHT FLAME

MOST HIGH ABOVE ALL THINGS, MIGHTY ONE

CONSOLER

COUNSELOR

FATHER, DAD

PROTECTOR SHIELD

PUPPET-MASTER

KING

WISDOM

SHEPHERD, VINEKEEPER

LOVER, BRIDEGROOM

CREATOR, POTTER

1. In the space below, draw a picture or symbol to represent God as you envision God now.

SOURCE OF ALL
BEING

ROCK

AVENGER

FRIEND

MOTHER
MOM

LORD

DIRECTOR

PURSUER
SEEKER

WATCHER,
SPY,
"BIG
BROTHER"
(in the negative
sense)

SPIRIT,
BREATH

THE HOLY ONE

2. And now, add to that picture some representation of *yourself,* that will show your relationship to God at this time in your life.

Who Do You Say I Am?

Down through history, people have thought of Jesus in many different ways.
Check the titles below that are most like your own ways of looking at Jesus.

BROTHER ____
SAVIOR, LIBERATOR ____
TEACHER, RABBI ____
FRIEND, LOVER ____
PRIEST, HIGH PRIEST ____
PROPHET ____
KING ____
GOD WITH US (EMMANUEL) ____
LORD ____
SUPERSTAR ____
HEALER ____
SERVANT ____
GOOD SHEPHERD, PASTOR ____
MESSIAH (ANOINTED ONE, CHRIST), SON OF DAVID ____
SON OF MAN ____
SON OF GOD ____
THE WORD ____
ALPHA AND OMEGA ____
LAMB OF GOD ____
COUNSELOR ____
SECOND ADAM ____

If you were to trace the story of your relationship to Jesus, what would you write?

Which Religion Is for Me? (if any)

There is the JEWISH FAITH . . . and its descendants, the CHRISTIAN CHURCHES . . . But among the Christian churches, there are *so many*:

1. the Mother Church or *Roman Catholic* Church

2. the *eastern Orthodox Churches* (which split off from Catholicism in the 11th century)

3. the *Protestant Churches* (which split off from Catholicism in the 16th century and after)—and there are almost *300* of these, ranging from Anglo-Catholic (Episcopal) to Quaker, with lots of other denominations in-between (Presbyterian, Methodist, Baptist, Congregational, Lutheran, and many others)

and then there are those religious groups or sects which don't feel at home with any of the Christian churches, but who are connected to them through sharing the Bible or belief in Jesus . . . groups like the Seventh Day Adventists, and the Mormons and the Jehovah's Witnesses and the Unitarians.

And then there are the other major world religions:

- ISLAM or the MOSLEM faith

- HINDUISM, the ancient religion of India

- BUDDHISM, the offspring of the Hindu faith

as well as all sorts of smaller groups.

Here are some of the reasons people give for belonging to one or another religion . . . or to none. Which ones make sense to me? (There is space to write in my own reactions.)

1. My parents raised me in the _____faith. I never thought about any other religion.

2. I'm married to someone of the _____faith, and I think it's best if everyone in a family worships in the same way, so I'm _____too.

3. I've studied the history of the _____religion very carefully, and it seems to me that it makes the most sense to believe in this way.

4. I very much like the way the people in the _____religion worship. It's a matter of style and taste which group one belongs to, and I've found the one that feels right to me.

5. I don't feel the need to belong to any organized religion. God is very real to me, and I find God in the world around me, in other people, and within my own soul.

Prayer

"PRAY PERSEVERINGLY... BE ATTENTIVE TO PRAYER... AND PRAY IN A SPIRIT OF THANKSGIVING..." — COL. 4:2

1. What is prayer, for me?

2. How do I usually pray? What seems to work best for me?

3. What type of prayer seems least natural or effective for me? Why?

4. Do I see prayer as something that I do?—or something that I am?—or both of these?—or more than these? Explain . . .

5. Do I have a favorite prayer spot? Or did I ever have such a place? If so, describe . . . Also, how did that place/spot help me pray?

6. Do I have a scheduled or routine time to pray? Would this be a help or a hindrance to my prayer life?

Some Pitfalls

The authors and those we work with have found it helpful to have before us a list of some of the many pitfalls encountered in spiritual direction—both by the persons seeking guidance and those accompanying others. These lists, which follow, are the equivalent to the markings of "Detour" and "Bridge Washed Out" on the road maps of outer geography. By going over them every so often, we are helped in our ministry, and we can also often foresee and make a little smoother some of the rough spots on the journey for others. This material is our personal compilation of the work of dozens of guides who have come before, in both the fields of ascetical theology and psychology.

Some Pitfalls for Those Receiving Spiritual Direction

1. *Seeking Spiritual Direction because it's the "in" thing*, or because one wants to be able to say, "I have a spiritual director." These egocentric motives, however, can be the door-openers to the higher motivation of desiring a closer walk with God.

2. *Seeking Spiritual Direction as a substitute* for therapy. Sometimes people who need therapy are reluctant to admit this, and will seek out the "safer" helping modality of spiritual direction. They need to be steered to good counseling, perhaps in tandem with spiritual direction.

3. *Handing Over Responsibility* for one's spiritual life to the director, dependency. "Tell me what to do . . ."

4. *Expecting the Director To Be Available at Any and All Times.* Every decision has to be checked out, every event has to be shared. The ideal is that a regular time and frequency of meeting be respected; this gives the person's inner life more of a container. Emergencies, of course, do come up—and we would want to be available for these if needed.

5. *Being Unwilling To Put Effort Into One's Inner Work,* expecting the spiritual companion to have the agenda for meetings and generally do the work for one. At the extreme, this develops into failure to show up for appointments or cancelling sessions for less-than-serious reasons.

6. *Hidden Agendas,* usually unconscious, such as "I'd like to get closer to this person and this is one way to do it" and "What I really want is friendship/tutoring/intimacy . . ." These can often be starting points for real work on the inner life, however.

7. *Expecting Instant Perfection* (the add-water-and-stir approach to growing). "Now that I have a spiritual guide, all will be clear sailing—sanctity is just around the corner."

8. *Failing To Share the Negatives* as well as the positives. "Our time together is supposed to be about uplifting things, so I won't talk about the crummy stuff . . ." or "I wouldn't want him/her to know this about me, so I won't mention it . . ."

9. *Seeing Spiritual Direction as an Intellectual Exchange.* "We talk about this idea and about that theoretical concept . . ." (but all stays above the collar and little or no growth takes place). God touches the heart even more than the mind.

10. *Possessiveness.* Attempts to "own" the director, or cultivate a closer relationship with him/her than he or she is open to. Friendship may, indeed, develop between two people in a relationship such as this, but it has to be two-way, desired by both.

11. *Bringing* Other *People's Lives to the Shared Time.* Sometimes this is a way of avoiding one's own inner struggles; sometimes it can be manipulative, with an eye to affecting the guide's relationship with another person.

12. *Staying with a Director* with whom there is no chemistry . . . or, worse, whose theology seems foreign to one's life, or whose own agenda gets in the way of one's growth. A somewhat critical eye is needed (especially at first) so that one doesn't idealize an all-too-human guide.

13. *Trying To Please the Spiritual Guide* by efforts to become what one thinks he or she wants one to become . . . rather than our own truest self.

We'll spare our readers the stories of how we discovered these pitfalls by falling into them ourselves, and continue with our second list (also compiled the hard way!) This one is even longer . . .

Some Pitfalls for Those Guiding Others

1. *Needing To Be Needed.* "Gee, I must be o.k. . . . look at all these people who want to come to talk to me." The emotional life of the helper centered in the helpees, who become one's main support community. This can lead to fostering dependency in them, hanging on to people when it isn't right for them, assuming too much responsibility for their lives (playing "Big Daddy" or "Big Mama", playing God). The words, "I don't know . . ." or "I haven't a clue . . ." are good words, as are the inevitable phrases, "I blew it . . . please forgive me."

2. *The Heresy of Good Works.* "I'm so busy seeing all these people that I haven't had time to pray or attend to my own inner life . . . I'm sure God understands . . . someone has to do it, etc., etc., etc." (The well soon runneth dry.)

3. *Thinking There's Just One Way To Grow*: "If I could just get _____ to read this book/start logging dreams/keep a journal/make a 30-day retreat (and so forth), I know all would be well."

4. *Forgetting Just* Who *Is Doing This Work*, which leads to thinking that one is getting pretty good at it all by one's self.

5. *Having Certain Subjects That Are Off Limits*, and letting that be known either by our own avoidance of them or discomfort with them when they arise. The most common are anger, sexuality, grief; our discomfort means we need to pay attention to the matter in our own life.

6. *Overextending, Not Setting Limits*: to the number of people in direction at any time, to the length of sessions or frequency of them, to being ever-available. Also, not giving ourselves time to prepare for sessions with others, not taking time to pray for them before and after visits. (This is related to number 2, above, and to number 7.)

7. *Not Knowing One's Own Boundaries*, which leads to taking on people one cannot work with knowledgeably or effectively, and getting in over one's head. This is the "Answer Man" stance, a perpetual hanging out of a "The Doctor Is In" shingle. Needed: a good bank of referrals.

8. *Forgetting To Evaluate and Pulse-Take Along the Way.* Many experienced directors suggest a trial period to begin, and make periodic evaluations with those they serve every six months or so: "Is this relationship meeting your needs?" "Do you feel you are growing closer to God?"

9. *Not Making Expectations Clear*, such as how one would like the other to prepare for sessions, what one would expect the other to be doing between times. Screening and ground rules are necessary.

10. *Giving in to "Blackmail"* (not a nice word, but sometimes a realistic one): "I need you," "Nobody else can help me," "You owe me your time/attention," "You're supposed to have the answers"—and so on.

11. *Minimizing the Dark Side of Life*, playing Pollyanna, trying to avoid pain and discomfort with chicken soup phrases like "It'll be better tomorrow," and "Every cloud has a silver lin-

ing." Religious chicken soup isn't any better than the garden variety (e.g., "God will provide" or "Just pray harder"—good advice, but inappropriate if someone needs to walk through pain or grief).

12. *A Mentality of Privatism*, which fosters a "God and me" spirituality that discounts both the church and the needs of the world.

13. *Fudging* on confidentiality.

14. *Being Naive/Untrained About Transference and Counter-Transference* and the powerful effects each can have in such a relationship.

15. *Undertaking This Ministry Without Solid Experience in Direction—and Without Proper Training and Continuing Supervision.* Better to say, "Sorry, I'm not ready . . ." than to be premature in leaping into this ministry—on the other hand, when *will* one be ready for such responsibility? And since spiritual companioning is as much art as science, how can one know? The best clues: that others seek one out, and that one has the covering of some representative body of the faithful (the latter is the outer call that parallels one's inner call).

16. *Failing To Provide a Meeting Space and Atmosphere* conducive to self-disclosure and prayer. This means both the physical setting and also one's own predisposition and readiness to receive others.

17. *Being More Interested in the Theory* behind another's experience than in the person. In the analytical process, this is sometimes called "analyzing the unconscious" (rather than the person). One may have brilliant insights into another's dreams or prayer life, and still fail to connect his or her mental abstractions to the seeker's life. This misses the whole point of spiritual guidance.

The list could go on, endlessly . . . trust in the God who is the agent of our deepening and transformation is the surest safeguard against our own head-over-heels splash into these and other pits. And the one most essential ingredient in that trust is that we are faithful to our own inner process of unfolding, that we continue to give top priority to our own seeking of the home within ourselves.

Jungian Spiritual Direction in Practice: A Personal Story

In closing, we thought it might be helpful to the reader to hear a little more about the authors' own way of practicing this beautiful ministry. For each of them it began as an "aside"; for Tom, an extension of his priestly ministry, which has been largely centered on retreat work; for Betsy, as an outgrowth of adult education ministry that focused on spirituality. Both of us approached spiritual companionship for others timidly, because the awareness of our own shortcomings and incompleteness loomed very large. (Later, this proved to be our greatest strength!) Of course, after many years of church-related work one learns that you're never *really* prepared to begin any ministry—but because the need is there, you go ahead and do it when the call is sent out. (And, if we waited until we felt we were ready, we'd probably go to our graves still preparing.)

From our separate associations with people from Jungian circles, we each had a definite vision of the ideal conditions under which spiritual companionship might be offered. The "feel" of many of the guides who come from the world of analytical psychology rests heavily on their providing a set-apart place—the *temenos* or sacred space we've referred to many times in COMING HOME. The relationship between the two persons is such a space, as is the actual place of meeting. Jungians like to compare both to the (closed) alchemical vessel that Jung himself referred to so often.

The major part of our time spent in spiritual companionship for others has been devoted to ministry to those in ministry—t.l.c. to those on the firing line in our churches and other religious institutions. Because both of us have been there for years, we know how much the front-line people need a place of nourishment and calm—an oasis. This is not to say that experienced people in ministry haven't learned to provide that for themselves; if they haven't, they usually burn out quickly. Our wish has been to supplement the lives of these busy people in as caring a way as possible. To that end and through the goodness of God, we shared ideas with several colleagues of different faiths who also had done and were doing their own inner work in analytical psychology.

The result is the Center for Sacred Psychology in West Los Angeles, California, a loose interfaith network of religiously-oriented therapists, spiritual companions and teachers who offer one-to-one time, small groups (on spiritual growth, dreams, fairy tales), workshops, retreats, therapeutic and graduate study supervision, vision quests and training. We have been able to provide what we think is the sort of oasis-place and caring deserved by those who come to us. One of the adjuncts we are most happy about is the abundance of visual materials we've gathered. These include a collection of mandalas for persons to choose from, to take home and color and live with (until their own inner mandala surfaces). There is also the sand tray, and an extensive archetypal picture collection with both color pictures in portfolios and hundreds of black and white drawings which are easily reproducible. (These are pictures of the many symbolic images listed earlier in this book, symbols of the basic patterns in the soul's life. At the end of this section is a copy of the flyer we give those who come to us which describes both the picture collection and the sand tray, giving them ideas as to how each may be used in their own soul-exploring.)

We also have art supplies at hand: clay, paints, pastel chalks, crayons, marking pens, paper and an easel. Some people gravitate toward these, to draw a dream image or to model in clay a shape that is emerging from within. They can work either in the loft which is there, or out in the brick courtyard next to the fountain; with our beautiful southern California weather, outdoor time is available almost ten months of the year. Recently, we have added a collection of paper dolls and buildings (the Emerald Castle of Oz, covered with green sequins, is one of these). These can be used in dry sand in the sand tray, and also provide easy reference images: someone who is trying to better know the sensuous side of his anima, for example, can find paper dolls of movie stars from which to get clues about her and also dancers of the past and present, as well as contemporary ordinary women. Handling the paper images can be the way of access to his own inner woman; they give even more variety than the sand tray figures. (There are even John Paul II paper dolls, believe it or not!) Paper images are less substantial than three-dimensional images, of course. They illustrate that in us which is just two-dimensional—or barely conscious. A fireplace and purring cat add homey touches to the Center.

The overall effect on others, when they walk in for an hour of spiritual sharing, is the feeling that they have come to a place where they can turn off their busy everyday life and all the mental mechanics which are usually part of that. The abundance of images says, "You've come to a place where you can have fun, where the child in you can come out safely and play, where the very serious business of soul-exploration can be addressed in a relaxed way." Our goal has been to provide mini-retreat time in this hectic world.

Other resources we have found which encourage people to discover and work with their personal imagery are:

• a research library on religious symbols, mythology and folklore and the arts. With this (and the excellent library at the Los Angeles C. G. Jung Institute nearby), we are able to help others track down and amplify their own personal symbols. When we do background research on a symbol (after the person has gone as far as possible alone), we copy our notes and pictures for the person, and also keep a copy for our own files in case another needs to learn the lore of, say, ravens or spiders or ziggurats.

• a tape and book lending library.

• a few books (basic Sanford, Kelsey and Johnson, plus Jung) for sale at cost, as well as large-sized blank journals, which are often hard to find.

• Myers-Briggs typology evaluation, and also natal, transited and progressed astrological charts, explained from a Christian perspective (which is 180° different from daily newspaper and future-predicting astrology, and close to the use saints Albert the Great and Thomas Aquinas made of this ancient tool).[20]

• help in understanding one's favorite story and how it mirrors the soul; we have a lending library of religious legends and fairy tales that have been examined and illustrated by both staff and guests.

• a set-apart cabinet for ritual-making ingredients: holy water, blessed oil, candles, incense, a blessing cup, even the book of the *I Ching* and three special coins (for those who understand how well this ties into any faith expression and want to use it as a projective tool).

• a small altar, and—on the walls—mandalas from many traditions. On the door, wreaths that change with the season (another mandala). These circles, and the several small carved figures of women from many cultures, say visually that our work focuses on the *feminine* energy, the neglected energy most of us (men and women) need for balance.

• special pictures (usually greeting cards) to give as gifts when the occasion presents itself: there are beautiful series of zodiac images, all of which can be "baptized" and seen as reflections of the faith life of all peoples (they haven't lasted thousands of years for no reason); there are also cards of the seasons and of the four ancient elements: earth, air, water and fire; there are special religious cards that make perfect mini-gifts when the need to celebrate something wonderful in the inner life occurs.

• finally, we offer those who come to the Center quiet time on their own on a regular basis. Often, the sessions of spiritual direction are filled to overflowing with gifts from the person's unconscious; they may never get to some of the other things we have made available, and the unstructured extra time alone allows them to do so.

We have also found that one other ingredient becomes increasingly important for spiritual directors or guides these days, and this is the matter of having good referrals. We may state very clearly to others—and to ourselves—that "I'm not a counselor, not a therapist . . . my concern is the growth end of the wellness scale, not the problem end of it." That is true. It is also true that those who come for spiritual direction—just like everyone else—will at some times have problems that need therapy or crisis intervention, and they may turn to the spiritual guide for help. We may find, as we grow more experienced, that we need to acquire paraprofessional counseling skills; our work may well spill over into pastoral counseling, and with the aid of whatever training is available, plus fine books like Eugene Kennedy's trilogy for non-professional helpers,[21] our range may broaden. Our Center has put together and kept up-to-date a referral file of people and agencies we know personally, and we now realize that the spiritual directors use it as much as the therapists.

Perhaps the best gift and aid we offer those who come to us is ongoing prayer. Each person is prayed for before they arrive and after they leave, and all (including former directees who have moved on) are remembered monthly in a special celebration. In addition, we regularly bless the spaces in which we meet with others.

Since all of us work in other settings as well as at the Center, we try to find ways to translate the "perfect setting and materials" we have put together at the Center into our parishes and other offices, most of which are shared space. We hope that by describing what we feel is the ideal, the reader will be able to do the same borrowing of ideas, if there are some new ones here.

Dr. von Franz, whose work is so well known, speaks of how the word "home" becomes a religious symbol of the Self, and of our instinctive feeling that we have an inner spiritual home where we belong.[22] It has been our great joy to write of our work in helping others return to that hidden-away home within themselves, and we welcome correspondence from our readers who are engaged in similar ministry: you can reach us at: Box 643 Gateway Station, Culver City, California 90232.

Two Special Ways of Soul-Exploration

1. THE SAND TRAY

At the turn of the century, H. G. Wells wrote a book titled *Floor Games*, about how he and his two sons made miniature worlds on the floor, using little people and construction materials. (Did *you* make scenes on Grandma's oriental rug? or sand castles at the beach? or house floor plans out of pebbles? or have a doll house?)

During the mid-1900's, several European growth specialists, most of them associated with C. G. Jung in Zurich, developed Wells' games into what we call, today, Sandplay. It is so simple—and so valuable as a way of connecting with our soul-life. (Fran Dora Kalff is *the* name in this field.)

A box is half-filled with sand. Next to it are shelves containing miniature people and trees and animals and buildings, along with small symbolic objects of many kinds. Following your instincts, you choose what appeals to you and arrange them in whatever way seems right to you—your inner voice tells you where they should go, just as a child knows *exactly* how his or her mud pie or leaf design should be arranged. The bottom of the sand tray is blue, as if it were water. In fact, water can be added to the sand, as long as paper or fabric or feathered articles aren't being used.

What emerges is almost always surprising! Our endlessly churning and analytical minds are bypassed as we, literally, play in the sand. The inner child in us comes out and plays . . . that child who knows the language of union with the unconscious—and with God. We "become like little children," with all the connection to our Inner Wisdom that implies.

In Jungian language, it is the Self that has been activated. The ego has (at last!) gotten out of the way so we can be sent the picture of a next step in our spiritual growth, or experience some needed healing, or sum up a phase of our inner life. We finish a picture in the sand and are amazed at the visual gift we have been sent from deep inside. The sand-tray image comes from the same place as the dream . . . and we can record it and work with it in just the way we would stay with an important dream. "What does it mean?", however, is a question that needn't be asked right away—the important effect of making a sand tray is experiencing the contact with the unconscious, a holy and numinous thing to do.

People sometimes bring their own special tokens or treasures with them to incorporate into their miniature worlds. When the sand tray is finished—and this may take from five minutes up to the whole hour of a session—the whole tray is photographed. (In the files a record of sand trays is kept in picture form [you can bring your own camera for your own record as well]: when a series feels concluded—perhaps after several months—the pictures can be set out and viewed as a whole.) The person may want to talk about a sand tray, or give it a title, either as it is finished or later (this is optional).

If we truly believe the kingdom of God is within us, this is one of several ways we can establish a link to it and dialogue with the incarnate God within.

The sand tray at the Center is available to all our regular clients. They often take one of the larger archetypal figures from a bookshelf in the office and bring that to the sand tray—a madonna, or a Sphinx of ancient Egypt, or a copy of Rodin's *The Thinker*.

After all, the inhabitants of the psyche are not all the same size! If you wish to use the sand tray, it helps to let us know before your regular visit, as our offices are shared. That way, we can be sure to reserve it for you. If you just have a last-minute, spontaneous wish to make a miniature world, it may be available, and you will be most welcome to use it.

2. THE PICTURE COLLECTION

At the Center, we also have a collection of pictures of a universal nature . . . Archetypal Pictures. Some are large, in loose-leaf notebooks; others are on sets of cards; still others comprise the collection of mandalas (the world-wide image of totality) that hangs on the walls. The pictures are representative of many times and places in the history of civilization, and yet the art and visual imagery of all peoples has always reflected the same themes:

Birth   *Going Home*
Happiness   *Resurrection and New life*
Moving On

Death   *Good*   *Evil*
Suffering
Standing Still   *The Masculine*
                              The Feminine

and all the other universal themes and images that transcend boundaries of space and time.

At the C.G. Jung Institutes in New York, Los Angeles and elsewhere is the ARAS collection (Archive for Research in Archetypal Symbolism). It is a resource of over 11,000 symbolic photographs and slides with detailed descriptions, which grew out of the famous Eranos meetings to which Jung was a prominent contributor. At the ARAS library, one may trace the history in art of countless images—perhaps the tower, or the bee, or the chalice, or bread, or the journey—throughout cultures east and west, from cave man times to space age art. It is the art of the collective unconscious. ARAS is a living, constantly growing art collection.

Our picture collection at the Center for Sacred Psychology is a mini-mini-version of the gigantic one at the Jung Institutes . . . and its purpose is somewhat different. The image or picture is the language of the unconscious, of the soul. Yet, we all too often find ourselves cut off from that language: "the words get in the way." Sometimes our dream life seems to dry up or we find ourselves living too much in the conscious world, out of touch with the realms within. Pictures can lead us back in at these times. We can just look at some.

At other times we may want to explore many versions of one theme: our books are arranged by topic (such as "Images of the Journey"). Spending time with a theme that is being sent to us at a particular time in our lives can deepen it in us. We look at the many ways that theme has been expressed visually and amplify its impact in our spiritual life. (Our collection, too, is constantly growing and being added to—we welcome additions to it.)

*Here Are Some Specific Picture-
Explorations To Try*

- Choose a picture you *like very much*—or *dislike very much*. Reflect on it. Write about it in your journal, perhaps draw it. Use the image for prayer, letting it soak down in you. Research it. Talk about it with whomever you are working with at the Center . . . in what way does the image live in you and reflect a part of your soul?

- Spread a box of the cards out on the floor of the loft at the Center. Choose three that stand for your past, your present and your future . . . or choose one that pictures your relationship to God at the moment . . . or select one that illustrates yourself at your best . . . or choose one that pictures your fondest dream or wish in life . . . or find the one that shows the greatest obstacle to holiness/wholeness in your life at this time . . . or choose the picture that illustrates what you would consider your greatest gift . . . or select one that shows what you would like to leave the world . . . and so on . . .

For creating your own images we have clay and art supplies at hand. Better still, can you provide your own at home so visual imagery will be a regular part of your life?

WHEREVER YOUR
TREASURE LIES,
THERE WILL YOU
FIND YOUR HEART...

— Matthew 6:21

Notes

1. See, for example, the basic text used in seminaries in the United States and elsewhere until not so long ago, *The Spiritual Life* by Adolphe Tanquerey (Tournai, Belgium: Desclée and Co., 1930). Based on the masters, rich in detail and resource material, this formative manual in ascetical theology makes the spiritual life sound like tough sledding.

2. *The Fire and The Cloud* by David A. Fleming, S.M. (New York: Paulist Press, 1978), is a good basic resource that shows the variety of spiritualities contained under the umbrella "Christian." For more extensive readings, see the Classics of Western Spirituality series published by Paulist Press.

3. Victor White, O.P. was one of the earliest notable names from the world of religion to dialogue with Jung about the implications of his ideas for religion; see *God and the Unconscious* (1952; rev. ed. Dallas: Spring Publications, 1982). In *Eclipse of God* (New York: Harper and Row, 1952), Martin Buber argued for the need of an "Other", a Thou. Jung's reply is found in *The Symbolic Life*, Volume 18 of the Collected Works (Princeton: Princeton University Press, 1976). See also Chapter IX of *C. G. Jung: His Myth in Our Time* by Marie-Louise von Franz (New York: Putnam's, 1975) for an overview of the Jung-theologians dialogue. John Dourley's paper focusing on the homecoming theme was published by the Guild of Pastoral Psychology, London in 1982. He is also the author of *The Psyche as Sacrament: C. G. Jung and Paul Tillich* (Toronto: Inner City Books, 1981).

4. These are only some of the better known names in this religion and psychology dialogue; it is a richly mined field at this writing (1985).

5. Again, this list only scratches the surface of a deep vein.

6. See *Spiritual Friend* by Tilden Edwards (New York: Paulist Press, 1980).

7. Both *Spiritual Friend*, and *Soul Friend* by Kenneth Leech (San Francisco: Harper & Row, 1977) give concise, informative views of the history of spiritual direction as a ministry, helping one see the many strains and flavors with which there are to identify. Edward Edinger, in an interview in *In Touch* (Nashua, N.H.: Centerpoint Foundation, Winter 1984), makes a case for the necessity of a strong classical education for Jungian analysts. Without this he says, one is divorced from one's own roots (and those of others). The same broad foundation is also a great blessing to those functioning as spiritual guides for others, and might include the natural sciences, philosophy, comparative religion, literature and mythology, as well as the arts and a knowledge of world history.

8. The best book available on spiritual guidance from a Jungian perspective is Morton Kelsey's *Companions on the Inner Way* (New York: Crossroad, 1983). It is a book that contains the rich fruits of this special man's life work.

9. A complete exploration of the varying ways of seeing evil is found in John Sanford's valuable book *Evil: The Shadow Side of Reality* (New York: Crossroad, 1981). See also Sanford's *Fritz Kunkel: Selected Writings* (New York: Paulist Press, 1984) and *King Saul, the Tragic Hero* (Mahwah, N.J.: Paulist, 1985).

10. This theme, of the Self "calling out" to the ego for a re-joining, is what Jung spoke of as "the religious instinct."

11. See Erich Neumann's *The Child* (New York: G.P. Putnam's Sons, 1973). Neumann has written at length on the way in which this stage theory differs in the lives of men and of women (in German; translated into English by Rebecca Jacobson in *Spring 1959,* New York: The Analytical Psychology Club of New York, Inc.). Were our simple chart to be amplified, it would include such distinctions; as it is, this chart is the basic "map" for people of either gender. In *Return of the Goddess,* analyst Edward C. Whitmont speaks of the new archetypal feminine consciousness now being born which completes Neumann's stage theory, just as shown in this chart (New York: Crossroad, 1982). He, too, is describing the return to home. There are, also, Buddhist systems which parallel this spiral map. See, for example, Lama Govinda's lectures on Pali Buddhism (early Indian) in *The Psychological Attitude of Early Buddhist Philosophy* (New York: Samuel Weiser, 1974). The Mahayana Buddhists use three descriptive terms that parallel Neumann's: "the person of little understanding," "the person of normal understanding," and "the person of superior understanding."

12. See Dora Kalff reference, notes for Chapter Seven, and Kunkel reference, notes for Chapter Four in *Coming Home.*

13. See Dr. Edinger's outline in issue No. 1 of *Quadrant* (N.Y.: C. G. Jung Foundation for Analytical Psychology, 1968).

14. *Ego and Archetype,* by Edward Edinger (New York: G.P. Putnam's Sons, 1972) p. 64.

15. See *Psychology and Religion: West and East,* Volume 11 of the Collected Works by C. G. Jung (Princeton: Princeton University Press, 1958), para. 758, and also para. 146, where Jung writes, ". . . what happens in the life of Christ happens always and everywhere." We must remember that the word "myth," in Jungian, refers to something "realer than real"; Morton Kelsey's succinct definition of myth, in his book on the story of Jesus, is "a story or series of stories describing man's contact with the world of spiritual realities which interact with the physical world . . .": *Myth, History and Faith: The Remythologizing of Christianity* (New York: Paulist Press, 1974, p. 4). On the ecumenical implications of this thought, see Edinger, *The Creation of Consciousness* (Toronto: Inner City Books, 1984), p. 32. This book contains an interesting chapter on Jung's *Answer to Job,* which, Edinger says, is an essay which cannot fail to offend almost everyone—believer and unbeliever! There is the sense that, while the Church has left the problem of evil in the realm of mystery, some of Jung's followers have become "more catholic than the Pope," and have concretized Jung's personal sense of YHWH into doctrine. This is still one of the border-skirmish areas among Jungians and the representatives of organized religion, just as it was during Jung's lifetime. Dr. Edinger's most recent amplification of the story of Jesus as archetypal story is quoted from seminars of May 1982 at St.

Simons Island in Georgia and January 1985 in Claremont, California.

16. The Psyche myth is told in *She* by Robert Johnson and in *Amor and Psyche* by Erich Neumann (Princeton: Princeton University Press, 1956).

17. See *Psychological Types*, Volume 6 of the Collected Works by C. G. Jung (Princeton: Princeton University Press 1971; originally published 1921), par. 708.

18. David L. Fleming, S.J. has an interesting comparison of models of spiritual direction and models of church in an article in *Review for Religious*, Volume 34, 1975, 3.

19. Dove Publications, Pecos, New Mexico 87552 and St. Anthony Messenger Press, 1615 Republic Street, Cincinnati, Ohio 45210. Still another very useful resource are the Scriptographic booklets from Channing L. Bete Co., 200 State Rd., S. Deerfield, MA 01373.

20. Both Albert and his pupil Thomas were clear about not using "the stars" to take responsibility for one's actions. As typical medieval men, they saw correspondences between that which is above and that which is below. As Dominicans, they sought *Veritas*—Truth—wherever it could be found, including the natural world of Aristotelian science and also the affinity with the heavens common to their time. Albert is the supposed author of a text on embryology, in which the developing child's qualities are assigned each to a different planet (see Louis McNeice's *Astrology*, a history of the ups and downs of this ancient art's respectability. London: Aldus Books Ltd, 1964).

21. *On Becoming a Counselor: A Basic Guide for Non-Professional Counselors, Sexual Counseling* and *Crisis Counseling*, all three published by Continuum Publishing Co., New York City.

22. Lecture #4 on Saint Niklaus van der Flüe, given at the C.G. Jung Institute, Zurich, on May 29, 1957.

My Own Experiences of HOME
● Quotations ● Pictures ● Dreams

My Own Experiences of HOME
● Quotations ● Pictures ● Dreams

My Own Experiences of HOME
● Quotations ● Pictures ● Dreams

For use by individuals
or in a group setting:

COMING HOME
A Handbook for Exploring the Sanctuary Within
By Betsy Caprio and Thomas M. Hedberg

The Handbook is an invitation to come home
and a road map for getting there.
Drawing on the insights of psychologist C.G. Jung,
the authors explore the primordial urge to "come home"
and the awful pain of homelessness.
Each of us, they conclude, has an inner place that is truly home,
but often we have lost our way to it
or believe its doors are closed to us.
The doors are not closed.
The way is not lost.
Anyone who longs to begin the journey
can open the Handbook and take the first step.

Available from your bookstore or from
Paulist Press
997 Macarthur Boulevard
Mahwah, N.J. 07430